RUN and not be weary

the Christian Answer to Fatigue

D0426505

DWIGHT L. CARLSON, M.D.

FLEMING H. REVELL COMPANY

Old Tappan, New Jersey

Library of Congress Cataloging in Publication Data

Carlson, Dwight L
    Run and not be weary.

    Bibliography: p.
    1. Fatigue, Mental. 2. Christian life—1960–
I. Title.
RC351.C27   248'.42   74–848
ISBN 0–8007–0650–1

CONTENTS

Part Five

The Solution (Energy for the Weary)

Part Six

Evaluation for Action

PREFACE

I have written this book to help sincere but tired Christians understand and deal with the ubiquitous problem of fatigue. Despite the fact that fatigue is a common problem among both Christians and non-Christians, very little has been written on the subject. There are short sections in medical books or journals on this subject, but where does the layman turn? Recently, I went to the main branch of our local library and found one book on the subject—published in 1905! Therefore, as a physician and a Christian I have studied the problem with the hope that the results of my findings will be of help to Christians suffering from unnecessary fatigue.

Sometimes I feel like an expert on the subject. I think I have experienced as much fatigue—severe, prolonged, and from many different sources—as is possible. But my experience is not unique. For many of you reading this book, fatigue is a severe problem. At any rate, I do speak from experience as one who periodically must reface the problem. I do not claim to have all the answers, but I have learned some lessons along the way. This book is the result of a desire to help the person suffering from fatigue to first understand the problem and its causes and then to present specific solutions available to him. Since I encourage the reader to be open and honest, I have endeavored to practice this, to set the pace, and to better relate to you despite the risks involved.

At the end of each chapter there are questions for individual study or group discussion. If used for group discussion, distribute paper and pencil to each person. Ask the group to answer the questions marked with an asterisk (*) on the paper without signing their names. Collect the papers, mix them, and distribute them again. Then tally the answers for each question and discuss the answers to those and the other questions.

The illustrations in chapter 17 are obviously fictitious. All other examples of persons and situations in this book are real. However, incidental aspects have been altered enough to preserve the anonymity of the individuals. Where this has been difficult to achieve, permission has been obtained from the persons involved.

I want to express my appreciation to Al Lunsford for initially encouraging the writing of this book and to Mrs. Donald Miller, Mrs. Charles Wiest, Miss Marjorie McClurkin, and Mrs. Dale Hansman who helped type the manuscript. Greatly appreciated were the helpful comments and criticisms of Dr. Kelly Bennett, H. Norman Wright, Rev. Gary Copeland, Rev. Randolf Klassen, Rev. Tom Collins, and Rev. Burton Swardstrom. Also appreciated was Rev. Daniel Seagren's valuable advice. Especially helpful was the editing by Mrs. Marilyn McGinnis which proved to be of great value.

Last but certainly not least, I want to express my deep gratitude to God for the tremendous help, encouragement, counsel, understanding, and patience of my dear wife Betty and our two great children, Susan and Gregory.

RUN and not be weary

Part One

The Problem of Fatigue

1

THE PROBLEM

They said I was suffering from exhaustion and the diagnosis couldn't have been more correct. At the ripe old age of nineteen I was utterly exhausted. The doctor encouraged me to develop better eating habits and gave me iron and vitamins. But the cause of my fatigue was deeper than simply not eating properly. Sheer exhaustion forced me to quit my job altogether and rest for a number of weeks.

The problem began shortly after I graduated from high school. I was very anxious to please God and felt He wanted me to leave my home and job and move near a servicemen's center a hundred miles away. To help my finances I sold the new car I'd worked so hard to purchase and by "faith" I looked to God to supply my needs in the new setting.

Eventually, I found a full-time job working as a mason's tender. After a hard day's work I'd head for the servicemen's center. I spent six nights a week, a half-day on Saturday, and all day Sunday at the center sharing Christ with marines heading for the battlefields of Korea. Someone advised me to take one night a week off, which I did, but instead of relaxing I went to the base and led a Bible study.

I was thoroughly convinced that a follower of Christ had to be disciplined. I stopped dating and had almost no social life; I worked hard to know all that God would teach me about prayer, Bible study, and I even tried fasting. Some challenging Christians I met encouraged memorizing three Bible verses a week. I thought if that were good, six must be better. So I committed to memory six verses per week, month after month.

About this time it was becoming harder and harder to get up in the morning for a quiet time. Putting the alarm clock in a pan across the room was no longer effective. So I hooked up a Model T spark coil with two wires across my legs in an effort to jolt myself out of bed at an early hour!

In many ways these were very meaningful days and God did bless them. Basically, I felt I was in His will and plan for my life. However, as the months passed I found that I was becoming more and more fatigued, and at times I felt absolutely miserable. I couldn't understand this. It seemed inconsistent with Christ's words in Matthew 11:28–30 which say, "Come to me, all who labor and are heavy laden, and I will give you rest. Take my yoke upon you, and learn from me; for I am gentle and lowly in heart, and you will find rest for your souls. For my yoke is easy, and my burden is light." Christ states in John 10:10 "I came that they may have life, and have it abundantly." 1 John 5:3 says: ". . . his commandments are not burdensome." For the most part, I really didn't experience this abundant life of resting in Christ. To this day I don't think I had any real insight into the basic problems I was facing. Maybe someone was trying to help me, but I didn't appreciate it if he was. Eventually, I had to stop work altogether and rest for several weeks.

Some years later I vividly remember asking a physician friend why I was often tired. He only shrugged his shoulders, which left me all the more confused. Sure, I could explain it if I had stayed up all night studying for a final exam—but what about all the other times?

As a practicing physician in Southern California, I've been repeatedly amazed at the number of patients coming to me whose chief complaint is that of fatigue. Some weeks there will be three or four patients with fatigue as a major complaint and several others for whom it is a minor concern. If the commercials on television are any indication, it must be a universal problem. Look at the companies who make millions selling remedies for "tired blood."

Fatigue can be defined as lassitude, lack of energy, weariness, tiredness, loss of a sense of well-being, and overall unpleasantness. Patients will often describe it as having no energy, no ambition, no interest, lack of pep, or just "all in."

Many physicians are uncomfortable dealing with this problem. Often the patient complaining of fatigue will receive a quick exam, some blood tests, a chest X ray, and then be sent away with a B-12 shot, a thyroid prescription, or be advised to take vitamins or go on a vacation. The more conscientious physician will do a more thorough exam and tests; but usually he will come up with "nothing"—that is, he will say there is no organic disease. If the problem is disabling, psychiatric help may be recommended, but to the vast majority often no constructive help is given.

It is easy to understand why a person might be weary who has rejected God's forgiveness and who carries (consciously or unconsciously) a load of guilt. All too often the Christian has not learned through Christ how to shed the same burden of guilt the world is carrying. As if that were not enough, he often distorts Christ's light yoke and makes it into a virtually unbearable one for him or anyone else. This is what the Pharisees did in their day. They were extremely religious and busy, but they developed a religious scheme which was impossible for them or anyone else to achieve. Thus they, and we, often fail to enter into God's rest. So the Christian ends up carrying even more of a burden than his spiritually indifferent neighbor. It's no wonder our witness so often falls on deaf ears—non-Christians don't want what we have.

These fatigue-producing burdens are not God's fault, they are ours. He desperately wants to help us rid ourselves of most fatigue. He wants to give our souls rest. The question is, how badly do we want rest, and what price are we willing to pay in terms of obedience to Him in order to achieve that rest?

If God so desperately wants to help us, why is fatigue so prevalent? One reason, I believe, is that if Satan cannot foul up the dedicated Christian through incorrect doctrine, lack of balance, materialism, laziness, lust, or other overt sins, his trump card today is fatigue and weariness. Ephesians 6:12 reminds us that our fight is not against a physical enemy but against powers that are spiritual and unseen. Satan, in fact, has done an excellent job in creating a pseudospiritual impression quite prevalent in Christendom today that if one isn't tired, worn to a frazzle, running here and there, one certainly couldn't be a very dedicated, spiritual, and sacrificing Christian. After all, if you aren't worn-out you aren't giving your all to Christ.

Too often we forget that the essence of life is more determined by the quality of life than the quantity. Fatigue usually adds very little quality to life. Psalms 127:1, 2 says:

> Unless the Lord builds the house, those who build it labor in vain. Unless the Lord watches over the city, the watchman stays awake in vain. It is vain that you rise up early and go late to rest, eating the bread of anxious toil; for he gives to his beloved in sleep.

The Book of Hebrews repeatedly speaks about a rest that we as Christians should be careful and, interestingly, *work* to obtain.

FUNCTIONS FATIGUE SERVE

"Is all fatigue wrong?" Someone may ask. "Certainly Christ was tired on a number of occasions." The obvious answer is no. Fatigue can serve some important functions, many of them good.

First of all, fatigue can be a FRIEND. At the end of a good day's work it is normal and a good feeling to be tired and able to sleep soundly. A lack of this kind of fatigue poses a real problem to many individuals with insomnia.

Also, fatigue can be a TRIAL. There is no doubt in my mind that Christ was tired on several occasions, such as in the desert, and yet this was a trial that God had ordained. Fatigue increases our susceptibility to sin, but God has promised us in 1 Corinthians 10:13 that He would uphold us in any such trial. However, we must be careful not to increase our susceptibility to sin through fatigue which He has not intended for us at that particular time. In such cases it does no good to blame God by calling the fatigue a trial from Him.

The third, and very common form in which fatigue exerts itself, is that of a WARNING. It says in *Harrison's Principles of Internal Medicine*, "The Psychoanalytic School of Psychiatry has postulated that chronic fatigue, like anxiety, is a danger signal that something is wrong: some activity or attitude has been persisted in too intensely or too long. The purpose of fatigue may be regarded as self-preservation." This kind of fatigue is like a fever. It's a warning signal. It doesn't tell us *what* is wrong—like a fever the causes are innumerable—but it tells us that *something* is wrong. A specific cause can almost inevitably be found if we start looking for it. If we don't, irreparable damage may be done before the underlying cause becomes obvious to everyone.

The last, and most serious, form that fatigue can take is that of an ENEMY. If Satan can only keep us tired enough, he can almost assuredly forget about us. Medically, certain physiological changes take place in the tired person. His work output is decreased; dissatisfaction and restlessness become apparent. He becomes unable to deal with complex problems and is upset by trivialities. Irritability, a critical attitude, loss of joy, and lack of spontaneity prevail. Spiritually, fatigue encourages doubt and depression. Remember what happened to Elijah (1 Kings 18, 19). We become extremely susceptible to sin in many forms that otherwise would pose no threat. Fatigue may also be an indicator of frank sin in our lives. Fatigue as an enemy and a warning signal will be the main consideration of this book.

DISCUSSION QUESTIONS

*1) Is fatigue a problem to you?
   a. almost constantly
   b. often
   c. occasionally
   d. seldom
   e. rarely or never

2) How prevalent a problem do you think fatigue is? Is it more common among sincere Christians or non-Christians?

3) Which group faces more fatigue?
   a. teen-agers
   b. young adults
   c. middle-aged people
   d. older adults

4) Is fatigue a spiritual problem?

5) Do you think most Christians' basic problem is lack of knowledge of how to cope with fatigue, or an unwillingness to do what they know they should?

6) Why do you think the author became exhausted at the age of nineteen?

7) Do most Christians carry the same burdens non-Christians do? Explain your answer.

8) Do you think many sincere Christians feel that they and others are not very dedicated if they are not extremely busy, active, and possibly worn-out?

9) Do you agree with the four functions of fatigue as described? List the four functions and give a present or past example of each in your life.

10) Is fatigue ever sin? Explain.

* See Preface, paragraph 3.

Part Two

Physical Causes of Fatigue

2

ORGANIC, CONSTITUTIONAL, AND PHYSICAL CAUSES

There are four basic groups into which the causes of fatigue can be classified. The first is ORGANIC, in which there is some actual illness or disease causing the fatigue. Second is the CONSTITU-TIONAL cause which is the normal variation of energy or work capability from one individual to another. Third are the PHYSI-CAL causes. Here the normal individual is pursuing normal activities either too intensely, or for too long a period of time, or too many different activities at the same time. The fourth and last group are those originating from PSYCHOLOGICAL or SPIRITUAL causes. These basically are inappropriate attitudes, thought patterns, or relationships which either should never have been allowed to dominate one's thinking in the first place, or which have persisted far too long for the well-being of the individual (and, often, for those around him). Some might separate the emotional, psychological, or psychiatric causes from the spiritual causes; however, there is so much overlap that, for the most part, I believe it is more appropriate to deal with them together.

ORGANIC CAUSES OF FATIGUE

The specific illnesses or diseases which can cause fatigue are legion. Almost every conceivable disease can cause, as a symptom, fatigue. The index pages of a several-thousand-page medical book would be an incomplete listing. Despite the fact that fatigue is one of the most common complaints a physician hears, less than 10 percent of patients seeking medical assistance have any organic illness actually causing their fatigue. Even of this 10 percent, many times only a portion of the fatigue they experience is due to the disease.

Some of the more common diseases that produce fatigue are *infections, endocrine disorders,* and *anemia.* Most *infections* are fairly acute and make their presence quite obvious, but occasionally a smoldering infection can persist for months without localized symptoms severe enough for one to seek medical attention. With modern-day drugs and medical attention this is much less common than it used to be and can be fairly well excluded as a factor by a good physical, chest X ray, and some urine and blood tests.

Metabolic, nutritional, and *endocrine disorders* are often implicated as the cause for fatigue. Patients and doctors commonly blame an individual's fatigue on one of these. *Hypothyroidism* (low thyroid) heads this list. However, it is a greatly overdiagnosed disease, and, in my experience, only a small percent of the patients that I see who are taking thyroid medication really need it.

There are at least four reasons why hypothyroidism has been overdiagnosed in the past. First, our tests were not as precise, leaving many borderline situations for the physician's best judgment as to whether or not the patient had a thyroid problem. When this fact was coupled with complaints of fatigue and overweight, two of the most common symptoms seen both in society in general and patients with hypothyroidism, it is no wonder the combination led to an overdiagnosis of this disease. Also, patients want answers and they are much more willing to accept a disease as the cause than to receive no answer or a long discussion regarding fatigue, obesity, and other problems. Lastly, the doctor often finds it easier to give the patient a prescription and tell him this will help, instead of going into a detailed discussion regarding many other possible explanations for the patient's problem.

Fortunately, when small amounts of thyroid are taken, a normal thyroid gland will compensate by proportionately decreasing its output of thyroid so that the patient remains in a normal thyroid state. Occasionally, however, we see a person who has excessive amounts of thyroid being given him, often to help him lose weight or to give him an extra spurt of energy. The symptoms of excessive thyroid commonly are weight loss, irritability, nervousness, palpitations, diarrhea, and sweating. However, lest we generalize too much, there are some patients who desperately must have thyroid to function normally. So be careful not to prematurely and wrongly judge either a person who is on thyroid medication or his physician.

Another problem called *reactive hypoglycemia* occurs occasionally and definitely can cause fatigue and several other symptoms. When a susceptible person eats a large amount of carbohydrates (that is, starches or sugars), at a fairly predictable time after eating these foods—usually two to five hours—he will experience nervousness, pounding of the heart, sweating, irritability, and hunger. Also, he may experience fatigue. Usually these symptoms will last for only fifteen to thirty minutes and then the body will compensate through reserve mechanisms by overcoming the drop in blood sugar which has resulted. Many times the person learns that by eating a candy bar or drinking a coke, he recovers more quickly.

Reactive hypoglycemia, in my opinion, is much more common than hypothyroidism. However, again we must be careful not to overdiagnose this symptom complex. Reactive hypoglycemia can easily be diagnosed by either obtaining a blood-sugar test at the time of the symptoms, or by having the patient take a five-hour glucose-tolerance test. During the test the patient is given a large sugar meal and then his blood sugar is checked periodically over a five-hour period. The doctor must find concurrently both a low blood sugar and the symptoms described, or at least some of them, to make the diagnosis of reactive hypoglycemia. The treatment is rather simple. A diet high in protein content and low in carbohydrates is usually all that is necessary. In rare instances, six meals a day are necessary. Most of these people have no further problem with hypoglycemia as long as they follow their diet. However, there is the rare person who will later develop diabetes, so blood sugars probably should be checked once a year.

Anemia is another and somewhat frequent cause of fatigue, especially in the menstruating woman. This can easily be checked by a laboratory. Some reports suggest that some women who do not have anemia but who have decreased iron storage in the bone marrow actually feel better taking small amounts of iron. If this is necessary, the very inexpensive ferrous-sulphate form of iron is almost always adequate.

Another common source of fatigue in our modern society is *birth-control pills*. This usually is very easy to diagnose because of the relationship between taking this medication and the onset of fatigue. Stopping the "pill" for several months may be necessary to clarify the point.

A woman may be slightly more subject to fatigue during certain periods of change in her life, such as *menstrual periods, pregnancy,* and *menopause.* She must boldly accept these changes. An understanding husband is extremely helpful. Let me quickly add, however, that menopausal symptoms are very real, affecting some more than others. Nevertheless, it often becomes the scapegoat for psychological and spiritual problems. Estrogens can help and should be used in normal doses in most cases, particularly if the patient is having symptoms. However, estrogens will not resolve the more deep-seated emotional problems.

Nutritional inadequacies are often blamed for fatigue, especially by companies profiting from this philosophy, or by doctors or patients who are unwilling to search in depth for the underlying causes. Though many in the United States do not eat as ideal a diet as they should, seldom are malnutrition or vitamin deficiency a problem if they have any regular intake of the basic food classes which include cereals, fruits, vegetables, meat, fish, poultry, and dairy products. Only if there is some coexistent disease will a person be malnourished even though he eats from these various classes regularly. Though additional vitamins seldom hurt, they usually provide an excess of the basic needs of the body and are excreted in the waste products. It is possible, however, to take too much of some vitamins. Excessive amounts of vitamins A and D can cause, in part, irritability, headaches, loss of hair, decalcification of bone, loss of appetite, an elevated calcium, and other toxic effects on the system.

These are days when we hear a lot from proponents of various diets. Some of this may have its place. The emphasis to maintain an ideal weight is good and also to decrease our total cholesterol and saturated fat intake. Too much cholesterol is related to increased incidents of heart and vascular disease. Many of the other somewhat fad diets are much more questionable, especially if generalized for all individuals. We emphasized above a high protein, low carbohydrate diet for people with reactive hypoglycemia. We also encourage this for diabetics or certain people with an excessive amount of some fats in the blood (technically called triglycerides). One might add to this list individuals who are trying to lose weight but, beyond this, it is questionable if this diet should be followed by the general population.

One additional comment about diet fads: most of these in themselves probably do not hurt anyone (especially if healthy and not pregnant) and certainly in some situations may be helpful. However, it is doubtful if this is an adequate basis to try and persuade others to indulge in your particular dietary persuasion. This is especially true if your enthusiasm focuses excessive attention upon this area and detracts attention from other areas which are far weaker links in the person's total development.

Probably the greatest nutritional problem in our modern society is too much nutrition. *Obesity* has reached epidemic proportions. It takes a tremendous toll in morbidity and mortality—it decreases the quality and length of life in untold millions. Many diseases are either caused by or adversely affected by it. A partial list includes heart disease, hypertension, diabetes, hyperlipedemia (elevated fats), and arthritis, to say nothing of the tremendous emotional disability affecting every thought and act of the overweight person.

Obesity also causes fatigue. Part of this fatigue is due to "postprandial fatigue" which to some extent occurs in all of us after we eat. This is due to blood going to the gastrointestinal tract and the chemical processes of digestion and metabolism. Latin Americans take advantage of this during the heat of the day and have a siesta. College students sometimes yield to the temptation to nap during their one o'clock classes, especially if the room is dark and a movie is being shown or the lecturer is boring. The point is, we all experience some of this—but the obese person experiences more. Also he finds that it is a lot bigger job to move around numerous pounds of extra adipose (fat) to say nothing of the emotional drain (see later chapters on unresolved internal conflicts). At any rate—obesity is a definite cause of fatigue.

There are other rare and somewhat interesting diseases which cause fatigue as the major symptom, such as *myasthenia gravis,* where, upon repeated use of a given muscle, weakness progresses eventually to the point of inability to use that muscle. This particularly occurs with ocular (eye) muscles but can first appear elsewhere and eventually may become generalized. Drugs are available for the treatment of this disease, but care must be exercised so that it is not overdiagnosed as it is a relatively uncommon illness.

Another rare illness is *familiar periodic paralysis* where discreet episodes of marked weakness occur. Again, this is of medical interest but, in the general population, seldom the cause of fatigue. This is not even a primer on the diseases that can cause fatigue.

To a certain degree, organic fatigue is present all the time and is increased with all work activity as the day passes. It is present when doing both enjoyable as well as mundane activities. If you have any question about the possibility of organic diseases causing your fatigue, see a competent physician for a thorough evaluation. If, after you have seen a physician, you question whether or not he's gotten to the bottom of your problem, ask for a consultation with another doctor. No physician worth his salt objects to your asking for another opinion if you do it in an appropriate manner. If, however, the second physician doesn't agree with your diagnosis, you'd better question your diagnosis. A doctor evaluating fatigue usually looks mainly for organic causes.

CONSTITUTIONAL CAUSES OF FATIGUE

Normal variations occur in almost every aspect of life. There are blondes and brunettes, tall people and short people, varying IQ's, and different physiques. Some individuals, unfortunately, face numerous medical problems. Others live to be one hundred without seeing a physician.

There are also tremendous variations in the constitutional energy levels from one person to another and the rapidity in which fatigue develops. My wife and I see this in our children. Our boy is eight; he wakes up almost instantly and needs less sleep than our girl, who is three years older She rises later than he, often taking a good thirty minutes to wake up in the morning. They both seem perfectly normal and well-adjusted, but their constitutional makeup is different.

Some individuals need eight hours of sleep a night and others do very well on five or six. To some degree this may be altered. I find that though I enjoy eight hours of sleep a night, I usually can function quite well if I get six to seven. However, if I consistently get much below six hours, the warning signs develop before many days pass. Some people find that if they take a nap in the late afternoon, say for a half hour, they can stay up a full extra hour in the evening.

Be honest and realistic about yourself. A person with an IQ

of 60 will never be able to keep up educationally with someone whose IQ is 140. And there are some who will never be able to keep up the energetic pace of others about him. Fortunately, God knows better than we do our energy capacity and needs and never requires of us more than He knows that we are capable of achieving. We, then, must accept ourselves as God has made us —with varying capabilities. We must be careful about comparing ourselves with others (*see* 2 Corinthians 10:12) and remember that many about us may be more tired than we think.

The wise person with less innate energy will know it, accept it, know that God accepts it, and avoid being chronically weary by setting appropriate limits on his activities.

But please don't stop reading here. Many who might quickly assume there is a constitutional cause for their fatigue may find the real cause to be discussed later in the book.

PHYSICAL CAUSES OF FATIGUE

Any activity or combination of activities which are engaged in too long or too strenuously will cause fatigue. These activities may be entirely normal in their own right. Here we are differentiating between fatigue caused by normal activities and fatigue whose primary cause is faulty attitudes or thought patterns.

Overwork is probably one of the greatest problem areas for dedicated, sincere Christians today. We too often are characterized by busyness and frantic activity resulting in fatigue and weariness instead of love, joy, compassion, and interest in others without ulterior motives.

Elijah in 1 Kings 18 and 19 is an excellent example of this problem. You will recall he was God's faithful prophet. He stood up against King Ahab who repeatedly threatened and sought his life. Elijah offered his sacrifice to God upon an altar saturated with water, and God sent fire down upon it to verify that He was the only true God and that Elijah was his servant. Elijah, then, had all of Baal's four-hundred-fifty prophets killed and subsequently prayed rain down from heaven. After such manifestations of God's power and presence, a woman, Jezebel, threatened him. Poor old Elijah became afraid, fled, and sank into depression so severe he wanted to die.

What caused this depression? There are several factors involved. For one thing, there had been a famine and drought, and in the long run that may have weakened the prophet. Also, God had told Elijah to go talk to threatening King Ahab. Instead, Elijah imposed on a friend, Obadiah, to go ahead of him to the king. One cannot determine from the Bible whether or not this was in God's plan, or whether the manipulation involved sapped Elijah of some of his energy. We find, also, that the prophet was totally unaware of many others who loved and served his God. He felt alone, saying, "I, even I only, am left; and they seek my life" (1 Kings 19:14). He then proceeded to compare himself with others saying, "I am no better than my [Baal-worshiping] fathers" (19:4). And to top it all off, he forgot God's obvious hand of blessing upon him and the miracles performed by his own hand. The last straw was the intimidation of a woman, causing Elijah to feel worthless and want to die.

How many of these things or others not recorded led up to his fatigue and depression, we don't know. However, we do know that God did not reprimand him for his lack of faith, or possibly many other legitimate areas of criticism. God's profound diagnosis was simple: "Elijah, you need rest and food" (see 19:5). Then he went in the strength of the Lord, and sometime later heard God speak in a "still small voice." Though God had business to do with Elijah, He had time to let him first eat and rest. There is no doubt that God could have given him instant nourishment and refreshment, but He didn't choose to use supernatural powers to remedy this natural need. The supernatural power involved to perform miracles was absolutely necessary to vindicate God's power before the nonbelieving generation. But it wasn't in God's plan and therefore was not to be expected or sought for Elijah's personal needs at this time, which were to be met by the normal, natural, God-given means—food and rest.

So it is with our activities. If God wanted to give us supernatural means to overcome His laws of nature—He certainly could. Instead, I believe He wants to give us strength and wisdom to live within His laws of nature. He could give us twenty-five hours a day to finish the many tasks that need to be done. However, the way human nature is we would soon need twenty-six and then twenty-seven hours in the day, and the basic problem would never be solved.

Or God could totally refresh the Christian after one hour of sleep and give us all bottomless pocketbooks so that we wouldn't have to "waste" time working for food and clothing. Think of all the extra time we would have to work in the fields that are "white to harvest." While He is at it, would it be too much to expect Him to increase our natural capabilities so that the learning and maturing process could be quickened? Then our life could be freed from many seemingly mundane activities so our productiveness for Christ could be increased. (I'm being facetious to emphasize my point.)

At special but probably infrequent times, God may choose to override His natural laws and give us supernatural energy. But for the most part God has not chosen to change any of the natural laws for the Christian when his spiritual rebirth occurs. Therefore we must learn and be willing to live under these natural (including physical, psychological, and spiritual) laws until we receive our resurrected bodies.

We must realize and accept the fact that we have as much and as little time as every other person has each day. This is exactly the right amount of time to complete every task He has ordained for us as long as we don't squander that time by self-centered activities. We often try and make up for squandered time by attempting to squeeze out of our lives extra energy to compensate. This leads to fatigue and abusing our bodies, His temple. Such abuse can be a form of yielding to temptation as much as it would have been if Christ had cast Himself down from the pinnacle in "faith" that the angels would protect Him from physical harm.

God has promised us all the riches of glory—but not necessarily now and in the manner that we dictate. It seems to me many Christians expect unrealistic special privileges and favors from God. After all, we think, if God controls the universe and extends such wonderful gifts as His Son, salvation, forgiveness, and so on, He can also prevent sickness, regardless of how I take care of my body, or whether I follow the doctor's advice, or miss sleep, etc. Certainly He can; but He usually chooses not to. That is, He expects us to live under the same natural laws as our non-Christian friends as long as we occupy this mortal body. Therefore, we must stop looking on Him as a magic charm that should make us immune to everyday problems and natural laws. Instead, we must follow Him moment by moment in obedience, utilizing our innate ability as well as His spiritual strength to deal with every natural and spiritual battle we face.

Addressing himself to the many demands placed on the Christian, Charles E. Hummell, in the *Tyranny of the Urgent,* emphasizes the point that so often the urgent immediate task which seemingly needs to be done right now keeps us going at a frenetic pace and keeps us from doing the more important task which God truly wants us to do. This urgent task may often be imposed on us by well-meaning Christians as we respond to needs rather than the direction of the Holy Spirit. Or perhaps our busyness is caused by ignorance as to relative values. Often, however, a person really doesn't want to slow down because the frantic pace meets a distorted need, or is a symptom helping him avoid or compensate for some more basic underlying problem.

Another reason we often live a frenetic, possibly good, and even very religious life, is because we are avoiding a truly spiritual life. It takes only a moderate amount of effort to live a good life by everyday standards and only a little more to be committed to a creed which is predictable. And in a sense our self, our plans, and our ego can remain king. We may receive considerable recognition and praise from our fellowmen. This, in fact, played a role in keeping the Pharisees from Christ and the truth (*see* John 5:44).

G. Campbell Morgan said, "I sometimes think that this is the pecular sin of the present age, the attempt to make up for lack of character by outside service." We can spend a fair amount of time theorizing and intellectualizing. It is easy for "older" Christians, as well as Christian organizations and denominations, to fall into this category if they are not extremely sensitive to the dynamic and sometimes quiet leading of the Holy Spirit.

A Spirit-led life freed from the frenetic rat race of our society must be totally committed not to a creed or program or goal but to Christ. Time, all our time, money, all our money, in fact, everything we have or are or hope to be, is given to a Person—Christ. Thus, we must get off the thrones which will make life less predictable, possibly misunderstood, but probably seldom hectic. We who are busy in religious activities must periodically ask ourselves, "Is religion, Christian service, the church, or some other spiritual endeavor or goal my god?" We are all capable of it becoming just that. Probably the greatest competitor to true yieldness to Christ is service for Christ.

Our modern society with its space-age pace, its computerized complexity, its subtle increasing standard of living and keeping up with the Joneses, has a slow but persistent way of eroding our personal relationship with Christ unless we are constantly vigilant. We do not need to prove our worth by our works; we already have it in Christ.

The ingredients for a frenetic, hectic, weary life are many. For example, unresolved personal problems or relationships, the salesmanship pressures of our age which often seep into the church, the feeling that this little good activity won't hurt anything, lack of time alone with ourself and our Maker, and failure to understand the grace of God.

If you are a *very busy person,* ask yourself if you are running from something, someone, self, or God? Or is your busyness the only way you can find self-esteem and worth?

Physical fatigue from the fast pace may be necessary and God-ordained at times in our lives, but it should not be chronic. It certainly can be a trial to endure. Remember, however, that one or two good nights of sleep with some time for reflection, meditation, and communion with God should totally refresh a person suffering purely from physical fatigue. If you aren't refreshed, there may be a psychological, spiritual, or organic cause for at least part of your problem.

DISCUSSION QUESTIONS

1) Why did an all-powerful God use normal means of meeting Elijah's needs of fatigue?

2) Do you think Christians often expect God to meet their needs and problems in a supernatural way when He expects them to utilize natural means available? Is the reverse true?

3) Why do you think many Christians are so extremely busy?

*4) If you try to squeeze extra things into your life, from where do you usually steal the time?
   a. God
   b. family
   c. sleep, relaxation
   d. others (list) —————————————————————

5) Why is it easier to live a good religious life than a truly spiritual life?

3

OTHER PHYSICAL AND
MISCELLANEOUS FACTORS

UNDERWORK

As you read the previous section you may have said to yourself, "Overwork is not my problem. I can't understand why some people get so involved." For you, saying no is no strain, in fact, it's quite easy. If this is your status, it's probably due to one of three reasons. You may at one time have been excessively busy and gotten weary and fed up with it all. Now you have gone to the other extreme and spend most of your free hours watching the one-eyed monster, or in some other unproductive activity. Or perhaps you run from the problems of life and normal struggles because it's just too much effort. You are unwilling to take the normal bruises encountered, so you withdraw into your house and close all the draperies, either literally or figuratively, to prevent contact with the real outside world.

Remember, the difference between the successful person and the failure is not that one has had more failures than the other, but that one person is able to learn from his failures and progresses past them.

A third possibility is that you have never seen the world and those about you through the eyes of the Saviour who wept and died for the needs about you. This reminds me of the attractive, successful, middle-aged lady, a patient of mine, who with tears says to me, "Dr. Carlson, every night I go to bed I pray that I won't wake up the next morning." Maybe there is a person like that living or working next to you. I could almost guarantee that you know at least a half-dozen individuals who act like all is going well, and yet these people are carrying heavy physical, mental, or spiritual burdens. But the callous person never sees them.

The underworked person with excessive meaningless time on his hands may or may not be as tired as the overworked person. But the lazy person will never have the thrill and satisfaction of knowing he is in God's perfect will. God can use a blundering saint but He can never use the lazy person who isn't willing to move.

The most vivid example of laziness and boredom I can remember was while I was in the navy and we were crossing the Pacific. Individuals who normally got along on six to eight hours of sleep were now bored, sleeping fourteen or more hours and tired most of the time.

In 2 Samuel 11, we read that though David's army was out in battle, and usually David was with them, this time he stayed behind. He was living a life of leisure and one afternoon, arising from his couch, he was tempted and with seemingly no struggle yielded to the temptation of Bathsheba. The results of his sin affected many lives and his entire future. We can only speculate as to how much his underactivity and avoiding the battlefield may have contributed to his sin.

The comfortable, lazy person is self-centered, unresponsive to those around him and, inevitably, to God. This tends to "force" Christian leaders and organizations to resort to salesmanship techniques to motivate people. The busy person often responds and ends up becoming busier. The lazy person often becomes more calloused.

Just as the excessively busy person must avoid that extreme of the pendulum's swing, so the inactive person will find his energy and sense of worth vanishing from him. As with so many things in life, there is a beautiful and crucial balance between these extremes. The lazy person may find that energy becomes available to him only as he gets involved in a meaningful task. He may need to commit himself to a project, if he doesn't have the vision to see needs or the ability to motivate himself to follow through on his own.

Our dear retired senior citizens are especially likely to fall into the trap of inactivity. They cannot expect to keep the pace of years gone by, yet excuses for inactivity often come easily. Some do not appreciate the fact that as long as God gives them breath, He has a plan and purpose for their lives. Along with this plan and purpose, they must realize their worth and value to others and their ability to help meet the needs of those about them. I know one retired businessman who has endeared himself to a small hospital and is now their chaplain, visiting and witnessing to the sick and needy. I have patients in nursing homes who would love to have someone come and extend Christ's love toward them. You don't have to look very far if your eyes are open and your feet willing to find someone in need of a cup of cold water given in Christ's name.

BOREDOM

Boredom is a major factor in producing fatigue. In fact, it is often a synonym for fatigue. Often the person who says "I am tired of this committee," really means, "I am bored with this committee," and may actually mean, "I am bored with the people on this committee."

A boring person fails to stimulate and makes others weary. If one is in the state of boredom—he has succeeded in boring himself. He has personally created so little interest in life that he has allowed himself to slip into a monotonous existence.

Boredom may manifest itself not only by inactivity but also

by disinterest and lack of enthusiasm or spontaneity. The bored person may even be excessively active. His hyperactivity may either be an attempt to escape his boring self or to desperately find meaning to life. Even many individuals with fairly "normal" paces, in all honesty, find life a monotonous bore though they are responsible enough to push themselves to do things that "should" be done.

What happens when a person is continually bored? With decreasing outside interests, an abnormal and distorted self-awareness often develops in the form of fatigue and psychosomatic illnesses. Many bored people turn their attention excessively upon themselves, their bodies, and its functions. The tick of a clock is seldom heard in a room where meaningful activities are taking place. But to a bored person sitting alone in the room, the tick may sound like a sledgehammer. So his bodily functions become all-important and psychosomatic illnesses often occur. An increased need for sleep, drug abuse, pursuing dangerous thrills, and many other symptoms or activities may result.

Other products of boredom are discouragement, disappointment, depression, negativism, and legalism. And strange as it may seem, these often lead to increased boredom. Thus the vicious cycle perpetuates itself unless the person energtically and boldly breaks out of this quick-setting mold.

Other causes of boredom are lack of variety (which is the "spice of life") in all of one's activities—including recreation, physical exertion, and relationships with friends. To be in a rut in any of these areas quickly constricts and limits one's energy.

One's attitude toward his activities is a great factor in his boredom. Many people get bored because they are afraid to launch out into new areas. They feel safe with the familiar, so mentally petrify in that state. They may have a negative outlook toward anything new, lacking a healthy enthusiasm. Often they are so rigid they may feel that a change or anything exciting or pleasurable must be sin. They are so inhibited they no longer appreciate the inspiration of God's wonderful creation whether it's a sunset, a flower, or a child. With this attitude, it's no wonder life is a bore and a drudgery. The bored person is actually slapping God in the face by unconsciously saying, in essence, "I am bored with Your creation and the life You have given me."

There is an inverse relationship between fatigue and energy, boredom and interest. To a large degree, boredom is caused by the lack of positive, stimulating, energizing, exciting factors in life. Also, often there is an excessive amount of unresolved internal conflicts in the individual's life. These conflicts will be discussed in chapters 5 through 18. The energizers which help abolish both fatigue and boredom are spontaneity and vitality towards life in general, obtainable challenging goals, purpose and meaning in one's individual life. These will be covered in chapters 19 to 22.

TIRED-HOUSEWIFE SYNDROME

The tired-housewife syndrome usually contains the ingredients of boredom, overwork, and lack of variety. Often the young woman who is now perpetually tired was active and free prior to her marriage, possibly with a profession of her own. Now she is married, "trapped" in the house with crying children, limited finances, and at the end of the day, a tired and often uncommunicative, unappreciative husband. With little intellectual stimulation, sense of purpose or accomplishment, she easily feels anxious, angry, and resentful which leads to fatigue, depression, and a host of other physical symptoms. The lack of exciting external stimuli in her life causes her to focus attention on the mundane—washing dishes, making beds, changing diapers—which greatly increases the problem. She may unconsciously develop the attitude of, "That's one less of the 54,700 times I have to do dishes in my life." This is not an exaggeration of the attitude to which many succumb.

This problem is not limited to young women. The problem has been characterized by age groups such as the "trapped twenties," "trying thirties," "fearful forties," "frantic fifties," and "sad sixties."

MEN AND MIDDLE-AGE DEPRESSION

Though I haven't heard as descriptive terms used for men, there are many men who feel boxed in on their jobs as much as the trapped housewife. They see little opportunity for promotion and the monotony of hours turns into days, weeks, months, and years. No doubt you have seen the eager, energetic, youthful man go through preparatory years looking to the future optimistically. After a few years on the job he reaches a plateau, becomes discouraged, and resigns himself to a life of unchallenging mediocrity. This problem afflicts all segments of manhood—the laborer and the professional, the irreligious and the religious, laity and minister.

A paycheck alone is never an adequate reward for one's lifework. A person's work should be meaningful and gratifying on many counts in addition to the money received. Ideally, a person should work at a job he really enjoys. If he does not, depression often sets in, particularly during middle age. The causes of this include the entire contents of this book; but, in particular, I believe it is often related to focusing all his efforts and worth on his work. More will be said about this in chapters 7 and 12.

MEDICATION AND ARTIFICIAL STIMULANTS

Artificial stimulants are another very common cause of fatigue in this age of weariness. The teen-age drug problem has its roots, I believe, in many of the things we are considering. They are often bored and want extra energy to continue a rapid pace so as not to miss out on anything. The mental stimulants are their attempt to obtain rapid gratification with as little effort and self-discipline as possible. When criticized they point to their parents who often are materialistic, self-centered individuals resorting to artificial means to solve *their* problems. The nervous request tranquilizers, the tired want stimulants, the insomniacs ask for sleeping pills, and the depressed want antidepressants. Occasionally, the same person complains of several of these problems at the same time.

Most medications have side effects. The person who took a sleeping pill may not be quite as alert the next morning because some of the medication often remains in the system the next day. Even nonmedicinal stimulants such as excessive amounts of coffee can cause nervousness, insomnia, and stimulation of the gastrointestinal tract. Let me quickly add, however, that drugs do have their proper place, and occasionally we have to strongly encourage a person to take a needful medication for a period of time. The person who is very anxious or depressed can profit greatly from the proper medication. While using drugs in their appropriate place, we encourage the individual to deal with the underlying emotional or spiritual problems producing these secondary symptoms, so eventually the need for the drugs will diminish. Sometimes this takes only a few hours or days if the person is truly willing to face and deal with the problem; other times the step-by-step road to recovery is longer.

DAILY ACTIVITY AND THE SLEEP CYCLE

A person's daily routine can also play an important role in his sense of well-being and susceptibility to fatigue. Definite hormonal changes occur during the day, such as an adrenal hormone whose level is about four times higher in the early morning hours than it is in the late afternoon. Our bodies need a fairly stable routine in order to maintain a normal balance. You cannot excessively alter this routine without feeling dragged out the next day and often for several days afterwards. If you've ever travelled across country by plane you will understand why "jet lag" takes its toll in our bodies. Crossing several time zones alters the body's normal routine and results in fatigue. Physical activity and exercise encourage the body and mind to sleep better at night and wake up more refreshed.

Many people wake up tired because they allow themselves to sleep poorly. How many millions of people in the United States toss and turn for hours each night I do not know. But judging from the number of patients I see each day who complain of this, the number must be appalling. Sleeplessness is a common partner with fatigue, anxiety, and depression.

If a person is continually tired and cannot sleep well, you can be fairly sure that at least part of the cause is psychological or spiritual in origin. Actually, all of the causes for fatigue that are not organic or constitutional are causes for insomnia. The poor sleeper is prone to be even more tired the next day and the vicious cycle continues.

Bedtime is the time the insomniac sets aside to rehearse and reflect on his problems. He engages in this self-destructive task either because he has some phobias about sleeping that have not been resolved, or because this is the first quiet moment he has had all day to reflect on the day. Or, more likely yet, the pressures of unresolved internal conflicts are too great to allow him to quietly go to sleep. Instead, they rear their ugly heads in hopes that the problems will be dealt with better than in previous attempts. Like a broken record, the insomniac replays the pressured thoughts within him—anxieties, resentments, bitterness, frustrations, financial and business problems, what-do-people-think phobias, guilt, and sins. These and many other internal conflicts will be dealt with in later chapters.

Stimulating and constructive ideas or plans can also rob a person of sleep. Occasionally they may be appropriate at bedtime, but beware of this occurring too frequently. I find if some new thought, or plan, or solution to a problem crosses my mind while trying to sleep, I am best off getting up and writing it down. Then I try to put the issue to rest or else I am liable to suffer the next day from fatigue and its consequences. The Lord wants to give us refreshing sleep (see Proverbs 3:24, Psalms 127:1, 2).

Besides insomnia being an indicator of our emotional and spiritual status, a few additional practical tips can help you develop good sleep habits. A satisfying day's work, especially if it includes some physical activity, helps you sleep better at night. Avoid taking excessive naps during the day and drinking coffee or other stimulants four to six hours before retiring. Stimulating thoughts, whether constructive or damaging, must be tamed by a certain amount of discipline to allow the switchboard of your mind and, subsequently, your entire body, to close down for the night. Quote Bible verses, pray and meditate on the wonders of God to help quiet your heart before God, and exclude the external pressures of the day. Some people focus their minds on something boring, like the side of a red barn, or count sheep to quiet their minds for sleep.

Mr. J., an elderly man, and his wife both came to me complaining about Mr. J.'s difficulty in sleeping. He would awaken about 12:30 A.M. each morning and said he couldn't fall back to sleep. He denied sleeping in the daytime and had as much activity as his health would allow. I was a little stumped until I questioned further.

"What do you do at 12:30 each morning?" I asked.

"Eat breakfast!"

"Who makes your breakfast? Your wife?"

"No, she doesn't get up then." But because he made so much noise rattling pots and pans around, she had everything set up the night before so all he had to do was plug in the coffeepot and other things and eat.

"What do you do after eating while the rest of the world is sawing wood?"

He sat in the living-room chair. No, he didn't watch TV or read. Did he doze? Well, he didn't think so.

"What time do you go to bed at night?"

"Well, I am so tired by 7:00 P.M. I can't stay up any longer." So he turns in only to repeat the above sequence.

The cause and solution is often not quite as apparent as in this gentleman's case. However, usually if we are willing to be open and honest with ourselves the cause becomes clear. And, unfortunately, like Mr. J., we often refuse to change our habits even when we know the solution.

Occasionally, the cause is much more elusive to both doctor and patient. Mr. and Mrs. R. first came to me as patients about three years ago. They had little use for God until about one-and-a-half years ago when he developed cancer. Then they became interested in hearing about God's love and plan for them.

I vividly remember the night I talked with them because I didn't get out of the office till after 8:00 P.M. I was tired, but felt on this occasion that God wanted me to go to their home and share the plan of salvation with them. Mrs. R. later said that she knew before I rang their doorbell that something special was going to happen that night—and it did! They both responded to Christ's invitation.

Mr. R.'s illness and subsequent death were hard on his wife, but she bravely faced it, has eagerly grown in Christ, and is concerned about sharing her life with those who don't know her Lord. She was doing quite well until just recently when she started developing several physical symptoms, one of which was severe insomnia which was not relieved with large doses of sleeping pills.

After reevaluating her for any diseases which might be causing her symptoms, I became quite certain that something emotional or spiritual was underneath it all. We discussed this, but despite a very frank and honest exchange, the problem eluded us both. Shortly thereafter, she spent an evening of spiritual sharing with my wife. Through this time of honest discussion it dawned on Mrs. R. that she had set up in her mind's eye the image of what a "good Christian" should be. Although she was trying hard and had grown a tremendous amount, she was still falling short of her image. She called me a few days later to report that since that night with my wife she realized that God accepted her just as she was, and she thus accepted herself. Since that night she has been "sleeping like a baby."

POOR ORGANIZATION

Jumbled thinking and poor organization inevitably will lead to inefficient use of one's time and all of its consequences of frustration, decreasing sense of worth, and fatigue, to name only a few. Some people have never been willing to discipline themselves and so seemingly thrive on one crisis after another. They create turmoil not only for themselves but for others. Poor organization can be as exhausting as the person who overplans and compulsively must carry out every finite detail. Priorities, proper management of time, and delegation of responsibility are crucial. Anything capable of disorganizing a person is capable of causing fatigue.

Procrastination also has its way of eating away at us. I find if I have unfinished dictation on my office desk, it can weigh me down for days until it's completed. Occasionally, it may be worth it to stay up late to complete a burdening task and sense the release and accomplishment it can bring.

A messy room or house, unnecessary noise, interruptions, or confusion can also drain a person. Some individuals overreact to all sorts of minimal external stimuli, thus living a battered experience resulting in fatigue. And like my elderly patient who continues to have breakfast at 12:30 A.M., most of the problems in this group persist because we don't want to change very badly.

DISCUSSION QUESTIONS

1) Why is it virtually impossible to get some people involved in meaningful activity? Should we push them into things?
2) How can the lazy person who wants to reform change?
3) What can men do to help their wives who suffer from the tired-housewife syndrome?
4) What can be done to help men avoid getting into the middle-age-depression syndrome?
5) Is it realistic to enjoy work? Explain what is meant and what is not meant by that term.
*6) Is insomnia a problem for you?
7) How do you solve the insomnia problem?

Part Three

Psychological and Spiritual Causes of Fatigue

4

THE RESULTS OF INTERNAL CONFLICT

A general practitioner recently referred a young lady to me who was complaining of fatigue and weakness to the point that she could hardly speak or keep her eyes open. The family brought her to my office in a wheelchair because she could not walk. I vividly remember several of us attempting to help her up on the examining table—an experience that seemed like trying to move one hundred twenty-five pounds of jelly without a container. She slept almost continually and actually *felt* exhausted though her problem proved to be psychiatric in origin. With appropriate treatment she regained her normal energy level in a matter of days.

Another patient complained of extreme fatigue although she was able to carry on her daily activities of working full time as well as being a housewife with several children. She was convinced that there was an organic cause for her fatigue, so we pursued a detailed investigation. After all the appropriate tests were completed, I told her I could find no organic cause for her fatigue. She became very angry and resentful toward me because I had not found some organic illness and refused to entertain the possibility that the problem might be psychological. I am sure she would have been more receptive to a diagnosis of cancer or some other dreaded disease rather than the implication of an emotional maladjustment.

Psychiatric or spiritually induced fatigue as opposed to organic fatigue is generally worse in the morning and may actually improve as the hours pass. Very often it is activity related. The tiredness is worse when the individual is bored and improves when the individual becomes involved in interesting activities. Fatigue from emotional and spiritual causes is just as real and incapacitating to the person experiencing it as fatigue produced by a severe organic cause. It is not "all in his head." He *feels* it.

Let's pause for a moment and remind ourselves that God has many laws in the universe. There are laws of chemistry and physics and various natural laws. We cannot violate these laws without suffering the consequences. Christ recognized and abided by the law of gravity by not casting Himself down from the pinnacle, even though the law of gravity was not described in detail by Newton until many years later.

Just as there are physical laws which are unchangeable and fixed, so there are spiritual laws and laws governing our minds. If we violate them we will suffer the consequences, whether we understand them in minute detail or deny their existence. In both the psychological and spiritual fields sometimes those who "know" the most about them are the least willing to apply them to their own lives. On the other hand, sometimes we see a poorly educated, often inconspicuous person who truly loves God and his fellowmen. With his rudimentary understanding of the Scriptures and common sense for everyday living, he has an amazingly full, meaningful, and integrated life.

All of God's laws are equally as reliable as the law of gravity. If a person sins, spiritual consequences will result. If he allows internal conflicts such as hatred and resentment to persist, they will eventually control him and inevitably cause certain unalterable results. These results may also affect other people about him, though he may never realize and associate the cause-and-effect relationship. Unfortunately, Christians are sometimes prone to think that they are not responsible for abiding by God's laws that affect our everyday living.

Fatigue often serves as a defense mechanism in the person with emotional or spiritual conflicts, allowing him to avoid resolving deep inner tensions. It becomes a method for self-preservation indicating the person's unconscious wish for inactivity. Instead of facing his problems and dealing with them, the individual retreats into a world of fatigue and sleep.

RELATIONSHIP OF FATIGUE TO ANXIETY, DEPRESSION, AND PSYCHOSOMATIC ILLNESS

Anxiety, depression, and psychosomatic illness are so closely related to fatigue that it is impossible to deal with fatigue without mentioning them. The basic underlying problem is unresolved internal conflicts which may originate from within the person, from without, or both. These unresolved internal conflicts produce pressure and if not quickly resolved will create inner tension that soon expresses itself in anxiety, fatigue, depression, or psychosomatic illness. Often anxiety is the first symptom to develop, but any sequence or combination is possible. These unresolved internal conflicts can also lead to other symptoms such as alcoholism, obesity, and drug abuse. Eventually, a psychosis (mental breakdown) can result.

Below is a simplified overview which helps us see the causative factors and the resultant symptoms. The symptoms cannot be

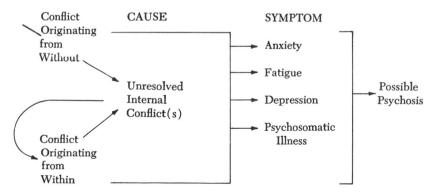

attacked until we first see their relationship to unresolved internal conflicts and appropriately deal with the cause. The basic types of internal conflicts will be dealt with in detail in chapters 5 through 18.

These destructive conflicts and symptoms not only sap the person of large amounts of energy, but they tend to perpetuate each other. For example, when anxiety continues, the psyche may try to reduce the energy to decrease the internal tension: thus fatigue becomes a useful escape mechanism to preserve the body.

The anxious, tired person easily becomes depressed, especially when all of his energy is dissipated internally and there is little left to pursue meaningful goals. Consciously or unconsciously, he may feel that anxiety, fatigue, and depression are not acceptable reasons for living an unproductive life. An illness (psychosomatic), however, is much more acceptable because it allows the person to withdraw from conflicts and gain attention. And so an illness develops. The person usually does not understand the cause of the illness, which produces more anxiety, and the vicious cycle continues. The original internal conflicts may become imperceptible and all goals, meaningful activity, and gratification are lost. When these stresses seemingly become too great to cope with, an unconscious internal mechanism may throw the person into a psychosis (mental breakdown). The further this progresses the greater the need for professional help.

The chart on page forty-seven shows how unresolved conflicts lead to various symptoms which in turn can lead to psychosis and ultimate loss of a meaningful goal.

It is easy to see why some people who have no other means of gaining attention unconsciously resort to attention-getting through illness, which only serves to perpetuate the illness. For this reason some people actually enjoy being ill, and it is virtually impossible to help a person get well who wants to be sick. Others do not want to be sick but are unwilling or don't know how to deal with the basic causative factors. Admittedly, all of this may be somewhat of an oversimplification, but is, I believe, basically accurate and very helpful in understanding the problem.

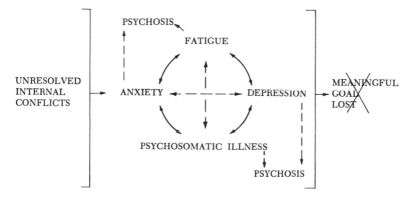

It is no wonder God's Word says in Psalms 107:17, "Some were sick through their sinful ways, and because of their iniquities suffered affliction." It is not surprising, then, that more than half of the symptoms that bring patients to see the average internist or general practitioner are a direct result of psychological or spiritual problems.

Now let us look a little more closely at anxiety, depression, and psychosomatic illness and their effect upon the body.

ANXIETY

Anxiety is characterized by apprehension, tension, uneasiness, or dread of impending disaster. It may vary in degree from occasional mild disquieting feelings to extreme states of "nervousness" which engulf the person continually. Especially in the more severe states, its uncontrolled energy seeks many other channels to dissipate its forces.

Anxiety is primarily of intrapsychic origin caused by threats from unresolved internal conflicts or dangerous impulses. This is usually differentiated from fear which is defined as a conscious reaction to a real danger—a reaction which is appropriate for the situation. By this definition, most fear in the Christian that persists very long either is actually anxiety or is coupled with it.

Just as fatigue can be a friend, so anxiety can alert us and prepare us for necessary action. Today I spent some time working on my car which is often a relaxing diversion from my work as a physician. After a couple of hours I realized I was starting to become slightly anxious. So I stopped and asked myself why. Then I realized I was spending more time on this job than I had planned and needed to stop and get back to some other unfinished work. As soon as I did this, the anxiety ceased.

One busy day, I kept a list of the times I noticed any anxiety within me, whether momentary or of longer duration. Then for each one I jotted down whether or not the anxiety could have been avoided or handled better. Some, I found, could have been avoided by better planning or preparation ahead of time, others could have been handled better when they occurred. Still others were part of the everyday stress of being a human and, on that day at least, I had handled them fairly well.

Usually we think of anxiety as a severe warning or enemy heralding persistent, unresolved internal conflicts. Sometimes the specific anxiety-producing issue is clearly known to the individual, but more often the specific internal conflict is not perceived. This is referred to as "free-floating anxiety."

The Scriptures aptly state, "Anxiety in a man's heart weighs him down" (Proverbs 12:25) and exhorts us to "Have no anxiety about anything, but in everything by prayer and supplication with thanksgiving let your requests be made known to God. And the peace of God, which passes all understanding, will keep your hearts and your minds in Christ Jesus" (Philippians 4:6, 7).

Anxiety is one of the ways the Holy Spirit uses to get our attention so that we can deal with some internal problem before it gets out of hand. When we pause and listen to Him with openness and honesty, He will readily point His finger to the specific area in our lives that needs to be dealt with. His desire is to give us deep, internal soul-rest if we are but willing to accept it on His terms. To deal with the anxiety will either mean taking some specific action or truly accepting and committing the issue to

Him. This approach will work for every unresolved internal conflict and will be dealt with in much greater detail later.

If the Holy Spirit does not point to a specific problem area, and we have been truly open and willing to get help if necessary, then the problem may be false guilt (see next chapter). Or the problem may have been so deeply repressed in the past that it is not readily accessible to work on now; thus the Holy Spirit is not ready to have us work on it either. (We must never use this as an excuse to avoid working on an area.) This also can be committed to Him for now and His timing.

The *iceberg principle* illustrates how I believe God wants us to look at and deal with our problems, especially internal conflicts. Only a small portion of the iceberg is visible above water. So also only a small portion of our basic inner unresolved conflicts may be visible in the form of tensions, pressures, or drives. Many issues remain, at least for the time, hidden from our awareness.

Just as we may send divers down to explore the size, shape, and depth of the submerged portion of the iceberg, we can investigate the hidden depths of the mind. (For most of us, however, there is enough to be worked on above the surface!) Through prayerful meditation, openness, and sharing with others we can be made aware of the problem and ways in which we can deal with it. As we chip away on what is visible, the Lord will cause the next portion of the iceberg to emerge for our attention.

Jesus told His disciples in John 16:12, 13 KJV, "I have yet many things to say unto you, but ye cannot bear them now. Howbeit when he, the Spirit of truth, is come, he will guide you into all truth. . . ." I believe He desires to work on our lives a little bit at a time and, fortunately, He knows just what our pace should be. If we refuse to work on a specific area that He is speaking to us about, no matter how small it may seem, we will suffer the consequences. We usually have little choice in what area He wants to work on next. Therefore, when anxiety is the Holy Spirit's means of attracting our attention to a problem, welcome it (*see* James 1:2–9). Listen to what He is saying and act according to His directions. The anxiety will then have served its useful purpose and will be quickly removed. Ignore His still, small voice and the anxiety will remain, intensify, and snowball.

Remember, Satan is often the author of extremes, but the Counselor (*see* John 14:26) will guide us with His supporting hand one step at a time. If we were to see all the needs of the world or our life at one time, it would overwhelm us. Unfortunately, too often sincere, zealous, well-meaning, but naïve Christians try and teach us all the truths, responsibilities, and obligations of a lifetime (or several) in a short period, thinking they are doing us and the Kingdom a favor. They don't realize the internal conflict and anxiety this can create, especially in the sensitive person.

One more comment on anxiety needs to be made before we move on to the next subject. Faulty thought patterns become a way of life for some individuals in particular; to a lesser extent everyone occasionally slips into this pattern. Recently, the husband of one of my patients aptly stated in the presence of his wife, "If there is nothing to worry about, she finds something to worry about."

Some people are continually anxious because of self-centeredness or self-pity. They gain a certain amount of enjoyment from anxiety although it ultimately costs them dearly. Some yield to worry because they have not found their purpose in life and thus have no meaningful, positive pursuits. Others succumb because they forget that the mind and its thoughts can never be a vacuum. If we do not actively fill our minds with good constructive thoughts (*see* Philippians 4:6–8) during all the free moments, the mind will take the course of least resistance and fill itself with self-centered thoughts which often prove to be destructive. Our minds are like a compass which, if working properly, always points north unless a magnet is brought close to it. As long as the magnet is within a few inches of the compass it will point to the magnet, but as soon as the magnet is removed the compass immediately returns to north. So we should apply our minds completely to the task at hand. But as soon as our minds are free, they should not spin aimlessly but return immediately to constructive pursuits and to God.

DEPRESSION

Fatigue and depression are often closely related because they have many similar causes. Fatigue may be a symptom of depression. Depression can be defined as a morbid sadness, feeling of helplessness, hopelessness, dejection, or melancholy. It can be a mild, brief occurrence or a severe incapacitating problem leading to total uselessness and ending in suicide. Its basic cause again is unresolved internal conflicts, including faulty thought patterns and loss of meaningful obtainable goals. These will be dealt with specifically later.

Anger, resentment, bitterness, self-pity, and guilt frequently cause depression. However, occasionally I believe depression can be a form of temptation without any root problem. If that is the case, we must learn to move through the depression with God's help and not to linger in it. We must stop our negative introspective thinking and act positively toward God, ourselves, and our fellowman. Spurgeon once said that depression came over him whenever the Lord was preparing a larger blessing for his ministry. He learned to welcome it as a prophet of good tidings to come.

PSYCHOSOMATIC ILLNESS

The energy of unresolved internal conflicts in a person seeks release. If not handled properly the person may explode with an outburst on an innocent bystander, such as a family member or the dog. Some would encourage yelling at someone or slamming a door to dissipate the energy of unresolved internal conflicts. This may be a slightly better method than allowing this energy to, so to speak, tear one's insides out. However, I believe, there are more appropriate ways to handle this energy. Irrational behavior can also occur without our understanding why we behave

as we do. For example, some external stimulus, though minimal
and inconsequential in itself, may touch near a repressed unresolved conflict producing anxiety and possibly some unexpected
behavior.

Anxiety is particularly difficult to live with for long periods. If
no action or the wrong action is taken against it, our unconscious
minds tend to bind it. This binding is the process of changing
an unacceptable internal problem into a physiological symptom.
These symptoms may be mild and transitory, such as diarrhea
before a college exam, or a severe, fixed illness which persists to
varying degrees even if most of the underlying problems have
later been resolved. Illness which is life-threatening can result.
Some of the more common diseases or symptoms which *may* be
an expression of an internal conflict are: dermatitis, asthma,
headaches, back and neck pain, and gastrointestinal disorders.

There are a variety of factors involved in the development of
a psychosomatic illness. Some are constitutional. We all have
areas of increased susceptibility to illness. The person with a
strong family history of allergies is more prone to develop wheezing or eczema, women are more prone to migraine headaches,
and the person with type-O blood to ulcers. But in most of these
diseases that often have a large psychosomatic component—for
example, asthma—a given attack of wheezing might be triggered
mainly by emotional stress, one time. However, another time it
might be caused by an infection and another time a very high
pollen count or any combination of these. And lest some of us
who are more fortunate and free from these diseases judge—let
me remind you that we may have more emotional or spiritual
problems without as apparent manifestations as our wheezing
friends.

Unfortunately, our highly stressful modern society is filled with
people who have many symptoms of psychosomatic illnesses.
Some people have one set of symptoms after another. Sometimes the individual goes from one doctor to another because
he really doesn't want to know the real cause of his problem.

A patient said to me the other day, "Don't tell me my illness is emotional. If it is, I don't want to hear it."

Much more frequently, people will use nonverbal communication to imply the same message to a physician. Naturally, these individuals are prone to develop organic illnesses. However, their history is often so crowded with numerous complaints, symptoms, resentments, and hostility, it becomes exceedingly difficult for the best physician to ferret out what is due to an organic disease and what is not. Thus, evaluation and tests are more numerous and occasionally the best physician will, for a while, miss an organic problem because the issues are so clouded. Another physician, receiving the clear message from the patient that there *must* be a physical cause, will *find* some physical cause—however minor. For the moment this will satisfy the patient. But it will also increase his or her hostility toward previous doctors, the medical profession, and the world, making it even more difficult to really help the person later on.

Fortunately, these extreme examples are not too frequent. It is no wonder 1 Corinthians 11:29–32 encourages us to examine ourselves in true honesty, for not doing so is the reason "many of you are weak and ill and some have died."

The attention derived from being ill tends, unfortunately, to perpetuate these illnesses, especially in those who neither recognize their own worth nor can accept gratification from constructive positive activity. Sometimes, however, the person with a psychosomatic illness may be better adjusted, harder working, more reliable, and easier to live with than others who channel their energies of unresolved conflicts into less acceptable avenues.

DISCUSSION QUESTIONS

*1) If you suffered from extreme fatigue and had a choice as to whether it was due to (a) serious organic illness or (b) psychological-spiritual causes, which would you choose? Why?

2) Can knowing the right answer or truths involved ever be a handicap in resolving our problems? Explain.

°3) Do you have unresolved internal conflicts? List several.

4) Do you agree with the author that unresolved internal conflicts can lead to problems of anxiety, fatigue, depression, psychosomatic illness and even psychosis?

5) You and several other church leaders have been asked by an ill individual to come to his or her house and pray for a miraculous healing. However, you have reason to think that there may be some major unresolved internal conflicts and wonder if the illness is psychosomatic in origin. At one time you had tried to carefully and kindly discuss this with the person but he would not listen. What should you do?

Part Four

Basic Causes of Internal Conflict

5

SIN AND GUILT

Our minds are a stage with an endless stream of thoughts playing for our attention—some good, some bad, and often there are frequent reruns. Sometimes we cannot prevent certain thoughts from making an entrance but we do have the power to let them play on or to throw them offstage.

The first step in sinning is to indulge in thoughts that are not pleasing to God. David did not sin when, for a moment, he saw Bathsheba. But he undoubtedly sinned in his mind, even before he touched her, when he continued to "look upon" her. (The Scripture account clearly outlines the steps leading to overt sin and its long term results in 2 Samuel 11.) Christ says that the acts of sin in our thought life are as sinful as the carrying out of the act (*see* Matthew 5:28). Proverbs 23:7 kjv says, "For as he [a man] thinketh in his heart, so is he."

Since the stage of our mind is a secret show (but not secret to God) we are tempted to indulge in many thoughts that we would never permit for general viewing. On this stage the battles that shape our lives are fought. Our basic unregenerated nature is self-centered and coupled with this are the evil forces of darkness (*see* Ephesians 6:10–18) vying for every opportunity to steal the show. The longer we indulge in a performance the harder it becomes to change channels before a passing look develops into a full-length feature (*see* 2 Corinthians 10:5).

Sin can take many forms such as breaking the Ten Commandments, especially the first two about loving God and our neighbor. It also includes evil thoughts, coveting, partiality, pride, greed, envy, jealousy, deceit, dishonesty, hardness of heart, self-ishness, self-pity, self-centeredness, worry, critical attitudes, resentfulness, bitterness, complacency, and grumbling. It may well, at least some of the time, include anxiety, self-effort, depression, irritability, self-consciousness, feelings of inferiority, bossiness, and manipulation of others. A. W. Tozer speaks of this in *The Pursuit of God* when he says:

> All of our heartaches and a great many of our physical ills spring directly from our sins: arrogance, resentfulness, evil imaginations, malice, greed—these are the sources of more human pain than all the diseases that ever afflicted mortal flesh. . . . The burden borne by mankind is a heavy and a crushing thing. . . . Let us examine our burden. It is altogether an interior one.

Most of our emotional and spiritual problems stem from sin.

Sin which is not properly and quickly dealt with leads to guilt and internal conflict. Any of the symptoms of unresolved internal conflict may result, including fatigue. David referred to his sin as a weight or burden (*see* Psalms 38:4) which I am sure contributed to fatigue. When one counsels individuals under great guilt they are often weary people. Anxiety and insomnia are frequently also present.

The solution for sin and the symptoms resulting from it is readily apparent in 1 John 1:9 KJV which says, "If we confess our sins, he is faithful and just to forgive us our sins, and to cleanse us from all unrighteousness." This verse means we must admit that we have willfully turned away from God's will to our own self-centeredness. This is basically what we do when we come to

Christ and receive His eternal salvation. We recognize our sinful nature and realize that the only remedy is made possible through the death and Resurrection of Christ, and we accept His gift.

As a Christian, however, I find that I periodically willfully disobey God and must keep short accounts, breathing a word of prayer to Him saying, "Lord, forgive me, I'm sorry." And then I go on. I don't think God wants us to make a production out of our sins. Rather, we should readily admit our need for His cleansing as soon as it is apparent. Sometimes when our children disobey, they readily admit it, say they are sorry, and within five minutes all is forgotten and life goes on happily. Occasionally, even though obviously wrong, they will not admit it. Instead, they throw a temper tantrum, cry, fight, resist, or wage a battle of reasons and excuses to explain their behavior or justify their actions. Such an episode ruins the entire evening for them and everyone else despite our best efforts as parents to appropriately handle the situation.

How many times do we as adults act like immature children before God with respect to sin? How many hours of grief and misery do we go through because we are unwilling to merely pause and agree with God's diagnosis? Brother Lawrence, in *The Practice of the Presence of God*, reminds us "that we ought without anxiety to expect pardon" from God (an act of faith) and that we should never be discouraged on account of sin (provided we are just willing to admit we have sinned).

Some well-meaning Christians with little insight, however, would label all of our problems as sin problems. This sort of counsel at the wrong time can play havoc, especially with a sensitive, sincere individual. At this point some reader may say, "That's heresy. All of our problems in this sick world are the result of sin." It is true that strife, sickness, suffering, death, and all other problems of this world are the result of sin—they would not be here if there was no sin. But on the other hand, you cannot properly deal with every problem by praying about it or trying to get the individual to admit his sin.

Let me illustrate. Mr. Adams was rushed to the emergency room because of chest pain so severe that it "felt like an elephant was sitting on his chest." I was called to assume his care. When I arrived his heartbeat had become very irregular and without proper medical treatment he would soon die. Now it may be true that he wasn't right with God. And if he were to die, getting right with God beforehand would be the most important thing that could happen to him. Also, hereditary factors and his loose living may have contributed to his developing the heart attack. But he sought from me medical attention, not the plan of salvation.

If that example seems obvious, let me cite the case of a young man who also presented himself at the emergency room complaining of dizziness and vomiting blood. Besides certain hereditary factors, an extreme spiritual-emotional conflict was certainly a major contributing factor to his disease. I might have been very spiritual and "right" by explaining to him that if he had not gotten himself into such a state of conflict he would not have been in this bloody mess. I also might have taken this opportunity to tell him that his basic problem really was a sin problem and that he should get right with God. But medically, legally, morally, and, in fact, spiritually, I had better not do that. I had better check his rapid pulse and his low blood pressure. Treatment had to be started immediately—intravenous fluids and blood while his life could still be saved. Even after the emergent things were done and his blood pressure restored, it still probably was not the appropriate time to talk about the causes that led to his bleeding ulcer. The ultraspiritual person might agree with these more obvious examples but have trouble with the numerous more subtle situations. Labeling and dealing with everything as only a sin problem is a naïve oversimplification. Sin was not the cause of all of Job's internal conflict. When Elijah was depressed he may even have sinned, though the Word of God is not clear on this point. Some of his self-righteous religious friends may have been ready to kick him when he was down even as Job's "friends" did. Perhaps it was fortunate Elijah didn't have any friends like that nearby! Our merciful God, however, did not criticize Elijah, but in love told him to sleep and eat.

We must be careful to differentiate between God's voice and Satan's. Remember, Satan is the accuser of the brethren, accusing them night and day (*see* Revelation 12:10). Unfortunately, sometimes people we highly respect may, unaware of what they are actually doing, create or perpetuate in us a feeling of guilt. Thus, we must make sure we are listening to God, verified by His Word, instead of merely self, others, or events.

False guilt often comes through the suggestions or advice of friends (like Job's) and is often related to taboos, social custom, or religious legalism. An example for many of us brought up in a strict conservative setting is movies. My church taught me that movies were anathema. Period. So I didn't go to movies. When I grew up I began evaluating that "rule" and decided that there was nothing unchristian about a picture that moves. Instead of pronouncing a curse on all movies, it seemed much more in keeping with Scripture to be selective in the movies one sees and not waste time on movies that were not edifying. After some struggle, I decided to start attending selected movies. Intellectually, I was sure that that was the right decision. However, on the feeling level it was quite some time before the feelings of false guilt went away when I did attend a movie. Those feelings of false guilt made making what I considered to be a more mature decision very difficult. I was dreadfully afraid the false guilt might really be true guilt—but at the same time I was sure it was not.

Leaders often are responsible for producing false guilt. A common pitfall is assuming everyone has the same needs and is in the same stage of growth. For example, the Sunday morning sermon is given to a very heterogeneous group of people. For many it may be exactly what they need as their next step in growth. But for others it may not be their need and without proper qualification may develop false guilt. It's comparable to my going to my waiting room and telling a group of patients with various problems, without first listening to them, what they need to do to get well. Can you picture the havoc this would create? Yet isn't this what we sometimes do in Christendom with tremendous internal conflict resulting?

Paul was very aware of creating false guilt in Christians and thus criticized other leaders who "troubled you with words, unsettling your minds." He avoided laying "greater burdens" than were necessary (*see* Acts 15:24–28).

In contrast true guilt violates a specific command of God, our prime relationship with God, or the rights of other people. False guilt originating from Satan's influence is more prone to cause a vague sense of uneasiness and guilt without direction.

If we are truly honest and ask Him to search our hearts as the psalmist of old, He most assuredly will. He will readily point His finger to *specifics* in our lives that must be dealt with. If, however, we have honestly sought God's face and He does not point out a specific area or make clear the next step of obedience, we had better question whether the Holy Spirit is doing the convicting. This does not mean that God will outline the whole plan and each step from the outset. It only means He will give us the *next* step. As we take that step, the following one will be apparent in due time. God eagerly directs us in specifics but often only one step at a time.

Misplaced guilt is, in a sense, a combination of true and false guilt which troubles and confuses countless Christians. A typical example is the sincere, hard-working, self-giving, but weary Christian who feels guilty if he says "no" to any opportunity of Christian service; so he gets busier and more tired and begins to doubt and question. He doesn't realize that his basic need, for example, may be for time in the Word and meditation or to admit a personal problem, need, or wrong attitude. The true area of guilt and need is disguised because he has not dealt with it. Satan, the confuser, capitalizes on it by misplacing it, making it more unlikely that the real problem will be dealt with.

No matter how long we have been Christians or how mature we may be, Satan's accusations, designed to squelch our joy and divert our course, will have to be refaced in a thousand different ways as long as we live. Guilt is an important reason for self-striving and frenetic activity which only complicate our problems. When we have honestly sought God and are convinced the guilt is from Satan, we must clearly label it as such in our minds and ask God through the shed blood of Jesus Christ to purify our conscience from this assault. If, on the other hand, guilt is a result of sin we, fortunately, do not need to live under this alienated uncomfortable condition. It only takes a moment to turn our thoughts toward God and admit our self-centeredness and sin.

Remember, there may not be much of a relationship between one's feelings of guilt and how close one actually is to God and His will. On the one hand, the hardened individual may feel little or no guilt because he has repressed God's voice. As he gets closer to God's penetrating eye, guilt may increase until his will accepts God's will and then all guilt should vanish. On the other hand, an obedient, sensitive Christian may be tempted by false guilt imposed by Satan through a doubt from within, or a doubt caused by a friend, a church or other group pressure, or circumstances. He may feel very uncomfortable, confused, frustrated, anxious, depressed, or weary until he listens to the clear though possibly soft voice of the Holy Spirit, recognizes the problem, and quickly deals with it.

The Christian life on earth has been likened to a pilgrimage. If we ever think we have arrived, or live that way, we are in for a big fall. As we grow, God's penetrating eye searches deeper levels into our lives to shine light on some hidden, previously unperceived corner. It is like a portion of the submerged iceberg bobbing up to full exposure. To continue in close fellowship means we must be willing to reevaluate any areas of our lives when they are exposed to new light. Each step takes a new act of obedience.

I vividly remember when I first invited Christ into my life at a church meeting and admitted my basic sinful nature. I was forgiven, filled with God's Spirit, and remember leaving the

meeting feeling like I was walking on a cloud. I held nothing
back to my knowledge and no specific act of sin crossed my mind
that needed special handling. I just admitted my basic sinful
nature. During the ensuing years my life was characterized by
periods of zeal to follow Christ, followed by lukewarm and even
cold periods.

I finally began to really grow and mature when I started
studying the Word. After several years I went through a period
of several months when, as often as I tried to draw close to God
in prayer, the Holy Spirit would remind me of three specific acts
of sin I had committed years earlier. I tried to push them out of
my mind, but when I was quiet before Him they kept coming
back. I asked God's forgiveness many times, but I felt in these instances I should do more than that (*see* Matthew 5:23, 24). One
day I finally said (and meant), "Lord, I don't feel I have the
strength to rectify these acts, but I am willing if You want me
to and will give me the strength." Immediately, I felt released
from the burden and internal conflict even though it was many
weeks before I carried out the promise.

When the time came, God gave me all the grace needed to confess a specific lie to my dad, admit stealing and offer restitution
to a former employer and also to the owner of a neighborhood
store. No doubt I have committed many other sins against my
fellowman, but the Holy Spirit brought only these three to mind
for me to deal with. If I wanted to continue my growth in Him
I had to be obedient. He has shown me that there is no need to
dig out every wrong act I have done in years gone by and go to
the person and confess it, unless He so directs.

On the other hand, as we follow Him in our day-by-day walk
He will often use people that rub us the wrong way, organizations that may not be sensitive to our needs or problems, or seemingly adverse "circumstances" to take off the sharp corners in our
lives and mold us into His image. Unfortunately, we sometimes
do not see His deeper purpose in all of these apparent problems.
It seems like about every six months God must work on some
rough edge in my life, such as an irritation that crops up, or

some bitterness that must be dealt with by confession to God and not infrequently to a person.

For example, recently I shared Christ with a patient of mine in the hospital though she was not interested in accepting the claims of Christ. Several weeks later I saw her in the office and became very irritated with her over questions it seemed to me we had discussed several times before or were insignificant to begin with. The curtness with which I ended the appointment and my irritation at her upset me the rest of the day until I said, "Okay, Lord," went back to the office, and dictated a letter of apology.

I am sincerely trying, through God's strength, to follow Him day-by-day and avoid situations like the above from developing. However, because I am a vessel of clay, it does not surprise me if occasionally I slip into some of these patterns, especially with the pressures I face from day-to-day. The problem is not so much that I slip and stumble. The crucial point is that I quickly recognize sin as sin and accept God's diagnosis, admitting it to Him and, if necessary, to other people who are involved; then I must move on in my life with Him.

Thus, it is evident that sin and guilt are major basic internal-conflict producers when we resist the Heavenly Father's message to us. All other internal-conflict producers are certainly "weights" (*see* Hebrews 12:1), at least, and in most cases sin. I believe, however, they warrant our discussing them individually because they otherwise may be overlooked. Some are subtle, others very commonplace and acceptable to our peer group. Many involve shades of gray which often hinder an understanding of their true significance.

DISCUSSION QUESTIONS

1) Do you think we actually become exactly what we allow ourselves to dwell upon in our thoughts? Illustrate. If that is the case, how do we change our actions? Our thoughts?
2) List the typical steps that lead to sin (2 Samuel 11). What

preliminary steps always proceed overt sin? At what point did David sin?

3) Do you think virtually all psychological problems are really spiritual ones and stem from sin? Why? Are there some that are not sin? Give an example.

4) Is it possible to be "too spiritual"? Explain.

5) Do you ever make too big a deal out of your sin?

6) In what ways do people and Satan cause guilt not intended by God? Why do people do this?

7) List the characteristics of guilt originating from:

God	Satan	Friends or ourselves

8) How do you deal with false or misplaced guilt? Give an example of each.

6

THE MASK

The mask is a covering to conceal or disguise one's true identity. It is a pretense, false claim or profession, a facade or front usually concealing something inferior. The mask may also serve as a protective covering.

Sin, guilt, self-centeredness, and pride almost always lead to a mask—putting our best foot forward to the point of hiding or at least obscuring our true selves from others. This, in turn, leads to hiding our true selves from ourselves, from God, and thus Him from us. We may become strangers to ourselves, God, and others without realizing what is happening. Consciously or unconsciously, this leads to a fear of being found out. And so the mask becomes a shield to protect us from what others might say or think about us if they really knew what we were like.

Like all other unresolved internal conflicts, the mask requires a lot of energy and leads to a host of problems besides fear, such as irritability, worry, anxiety, fatigue, excusing ourselves, blaming others, and, not infrequently, frank lying and deceit.

Unconfessed sin is the only thing we have to be ashamed of. If we would only stop pretending and accept God's evaluation

of us that we are nothing apart from Him but have everything
with Him, then we can start to bring harmony to the person inside and the personage that people see. Now the energy—once
used to maintain a mask—can be distributed in useful tasks.
Many authors, such as Paul Tournier, Roy Hession, and Keith
Miller have aptly dealt with this issue.

Unconfessed sin in all people—whether Christian or non-Christian—usually leads to hiding oneself from God and others. However, the problem of the mask is sometimes greater among religious individuals because they have a standard to live up to.
Speaking to the religious leaders of His day, Christ said, "Alas for
you, you hypocritical scribes and Pharisees! You are like white-
washed tombs, which look fine on the outside but inside are full
of dead men's bones and all kinds of rottenness. For you appear
like good men on the outside—but inside you are a mass of pretense and wickedness" (Matthew 23:27, 28 PHILLIPS). And after
a similar indictment ". . . one of the experts in the Law said to
him, 'Master, when you say things like this, you are insulting us
as well.' And he returned: 'Yes, and I do blame you experts in
the Law! For you pile up back-breaking burdens for men to
bear . . .'" (Luke 11:45, 46 PHILLIPS). As I have talked with and
observed numerous individuals in the office, church, or society,
I am convinced that the mask causes internal burdens resulting
in various symptoms including fatigue. For many it is only a
small contributing factor. For a few it is a gigantic load.

When we refuse to remove our masks, we not only create internal conflict and fatigue, but we also hinder our own growth
and the growth of others. Individuals grow by relating to other
genuine people and seeing how they deal with life's problems.
Christian leaders must be willing to first remove their own masks
before they can ever expect others to do likewise. Only as we
Christians are willing to expose our feet of clay will others feel
(and maybe only then be) safe to expose themselves and their
needs.

Most of us maintain the mask in order to hide our sin and also
because we fear possible loss of prestige and "hurt" from others

if we expose ourselves. We may also be unwilling to grow which exposing ourselves would produce. Or perhaps we are unwilling to admit our continual need for God or our need for other human beings to help us grow.

Two misconceptions foster maintaining the mask: fear that the truth about us will hurt our testimony and thus the gospel and the Lord, and the misconception that the abundant life means a life without problems.

To those who would say that exposing themselves might hurt their testimony, let me remind you of 1 Peter 4:17 KJV which says, "For the time is come that judgment must begin at the house of God: and if it first begin at us, what shall the end be of them that obey not the gospel of God?" If a Christian leader is living a life of pretense it is most likely (despite the seeming results he may proudly point to) his life is accomplishing very little of eternal value. It may even be hindering God's work in the lives of people around him. God's plan and desire is that we honestly and openly recognize who and what we are—imperfect vessels of clay. Then we must actively rely on and follow Him, as He gives strength to help us work on our imperfections. Only in this way will our lives have eternal significance and glorify God and the gospel be furthered. This is often the means God uses to start revival.

On a few rare occasions I have seen individuals swing to the opposite extreme and always put their *worst* foot forward. This can cause havoc to the individual and to others. Either extreme, putting only our good or bad foot forward, is unwise. God does not want us to use up precious energy extending *either* foot; rather we should simply be genuine, transparent, real individuals before God, others, and ourselves.

Let me also comment briefly about the second misconception —that the abundant life means one free of problems. If not resolved, this misconception can cause internal problems and lead to pretense, doubt, despair, and even rejection of the Christian life.

Some people have the mistaken idea that once they have

accepted Christ they will have a happy, carefree life, free of all struggles. From the eternal perspective, God promises to give every believer life abundantly. So much of our struggling, grief, and illnesses are a direct result of our sin—our refusal to die to self (see 1 Corinthians 15:31) and make Christ the Lord of our life. The carnal Christian's internal struggles may actually increase until he makes Christ Lord of all. God wants to deliver us from these struggles and replace them with His fullness, joy, and inner peace. This can only be done as we take up our cross and follow Him.

God promises an abundant life within. This can be reached as our internal struggles and conflicts are diminished and our eternal position with God is realized. When we thus experience Christ's love, it may flow through us in such a way as to actually decrease the conflicts with the world. However, there is no guarantee of this as the world is hostile against Christ and our conflicts may actually increase if we are truly obedient to God. The whole New Testament verifies this, such as Paul's comment in 2 Corinthians 6:10 KJV: "As sorrowful, yet alway rejoicing; as poor, yet making many rich; as having nothing, and yet possessing all things."

One word of warning: some religious person might use my statements to justify the heavy loads he is imposing on others which rob them of their joy in Christ. Remember 1 John 5:3 which says, ". . . his commandments are not burdensome" or "grievous." Satan, as usual, is the author of extremes. He would either like us to be happy-go-lucky, indifferent Christians or else carrying an awful, dreaded, heavy burden, making the Christian life a real drag.

How does one take off his mask? It's not just a simple matter of slipping the rubber bands off from behind your ears and dropping the mask to the ground. It's especially difficult if it's been in long and continuous use so that it tightly adheres to the face, making its removal painful—but only briefly. Then there is the fear of exposing ourselves. We are frightened about what we might see and the repercussions when others see us as we are. To overcome these resisting forces we must first be willing to admit that we are wearing a mask. This is very difficult for many because they have even disguised it from themselves. So they may have to start with the prayer: "Lord, am I wearing a mask?" Once admitting to ourselves that we are wearing a mask, we must be willing to admit its presence to God. We must realize that it is deceitful—which is sin. It's really a matter of surrendering this area of our lives to God.

Truly realizing the devastating effects the mask is having on us and those about us also helps us remove the mask—when you realize it need not remain, you catch a glimpse of the possible you, without a mask.

Having admitted to yourself and God the presence of a mask, the next step is to find a friend or small group you feel safe with. Decide that at the appropriate time you will start exposing your real self. Soon you will be more comfortable with your new true self and the honest transparent relationship will spread. Removing the mask may bring to light some other areas that need to be worked on such as guilt, inadequacy, bitterness, or people pleasing. You must be willing to work on these areas as God directs if you want to keep the mask off.

One word of caution. Taking the mask off does not mean you should purposefully, forcefully expose every aspect of your life to everyone around you. There are times when this may not only serve no useful function but actually be damaging and unloving to others or yourself. It does, however, mean that you *must be willing* to expose any area God should indicate needs exposing. It also means that at all times you must portray a true representation of your deeper self. You must never be phony.

DISCUSSION QUESTIONS

*1) Do you often wear a mask to conceal your deeper, real self?
*2) Do you really want to wear a mask?
*3) Do you think that the mask is common among the people with whom you fellowship?

4) Do you think that religious people tend to wear a mask more often than the nonreligious? Why?

5) List ten results of wearing a mask and hiding one's real self.

*6) Is there anyone you feel safe with and are able to share with on a truly deep level?

*7) Do you want a deep, open, transparent, sharing relationship with at least one other individual? Why might a person answer no to this?

8) What is your definition of the abundant life? What does it mean and what does it not mean?

9) Is Satan ever the originator of the question, "Are you willing to be a fool for Christ?"

*10) Do you really want non-Christians to have the life you have, just the way you have it now?

11) Isn't it inconsistent to say we don't have to reveal everything about ourselves when we remove our mask? How do you decide what to reveal?

12) What should you do if you have tried to remove your mask but a friend or small group hurt you?

13) What specifically have you done to try and remove your mask?

7

INADEQUACY

Today a patient complaining of fatigue told me that there has only been one person in all of his life who ever made him feel he was "worth anything." That was another doctor. If everyone were as honest as that man we would probably find that deep feelings of inadequacy, inferiority, and insecurity are epidemic. Even feelings of total worthlessness are not rare.

I am repeatedly amazed as I get to know prominent successful individuals and realize that in the quietness of their hearts there is a tremendous feeling of inadequacy. In an anonymous questionnaire of a basically healthy, upper-middle-class group of people, 50 percent answered they "*often* felt inadequate, inferior or worthless."

Few people are able to properly evaluate themselves. Some are overconfident, but far more common are those who feel inferior. These feelings of inadequacy, inferiority, insecurity, or worthlessness readily lead to internal conflict which may contribute substantially to producing fatigue. It may also result in anxiety, depression, and psychosomatic illnesses, cause the person to put on a mask, become irritable and critical, or a people pleaser, to name a few.

We typically think of inadequacy manifesting itself in timidity, indecisiveness, self-defacing behavior. However, excusing ourselves, frantic striving, dogmatic behavior, bossiness, and extreme perfection can equally be manifestations of this malady. The insecure person with his increased fear and anxiety tends to increase his likelihood of failure. And even if he should succeed in overcompensating, he tends to belittle his work unless the basic causes are properly appreciated and dealt with.

What are the primary causes of inadequate feelings? How does inadequacy begin? Basic to this whole problem is the fact that we all are, in fact, inadequate. From the eternal-absolute perspective, we will never measure up. It is true that the more successful person will be more prone to gain a measure of value, worth, significance, and a feeling of adequacy. This may readily lead to pride, self-sufficiency, and arrogance. A fairly competent person may live in this state virtually all his life.

I am reminded of a patient in his seventies who claimed to be totally satisfied with his life. Everything seemed to be going well for him without apparent feelings of inadequacy. I tried to share the gospel with him, but he had no use for spiritual things and no apparent need; he was very self-confident. I continued to see him for various medical problems, though he would not follow recommendations very well. Then one day he developed lung cancer. How vividly I remember him saying to me with slurred speech, "Why me, why me, why did this happen to me?" With tears he apparently had never shed in his adult life, he could not understand why he should be dying.

To me this points out the ultimate inadequacy of all humans. If we are honest we instinctively realize our frailties, though we may never admit them. This might be diagramed as follows:

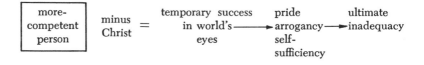

The less competent or successful person is acutely aware of the competitiveness of the world and possibly has a series of defeats which may overwhelm him to the point of feeling worthless. This readily leads to internal conflict and its various manifestations including fatigue. This may be diagramed as follows:

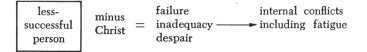

What then tends to make finite humans prone to developing feelings of inadequacy? First of all, I believe our basic innate abilities play a significant role in the pathogenesis. The person with the high IQ, good health, and an attractive appearance is endowed with a plus factor right from the start. The individual without these innate assets is handicapped right from the start.

Second, the self-image imparted to us by others has a tremendous effect in molding our feelings of worth. Parents, teachers, friends, and peers who properly encourage us and convey to us appropriate feelings of worth lay an invaluable foundation for future years.

Third, opportunities and a proper growth pattern are essential. Life is a series of steps. One successfully completes the first grade before going to the second grade. If a child is given too many tasks beyond his reach he may soon give up and feel inadequate.

The fourth cause in developing inadequacies is improper comparisons and evaluations both by ourselves and others. For example, if a new housewife and mother compares herself with Mrs. Jones who is an outstanding cook, Miss Smith who just won a beauty contest, and Mrs. Johnson who is a teacher and expert in handling children, she undoubtedly will come out on the short end. Many individuals compare themselves with the outstanding qualities in other people, often even overestimating those qualities. They fail to see that those individuals have many weak areas and often underestimate their own abilities.

The fifth frequent cause of inadequacies is dwelling on past failures and defeats. Such conditioning of the mind will inevitably lead to throwing in the sponge.

Sixth, some people feel inadequate because of improper job placement. Many jobs require a certain innate ability, skill, or interest which not everyone has or ever will obtain. Many are propelled into positions or jobs unsuited for them by parents, counselors, or their own poor judgment. It was never intended by God and as long as they remain in it they will never *be* adequate. In this situation inadequacy is an inevitable secondary result. Only by dealing with the primary problem will the symptom be abolished.

The seventh and last cause is inadequate preparation or training. Some people are just plain lazy. A student who fails to study should not be surprised if he fails a course. Some people go through life with a series of such failures and it is understandable why they feel inadequate.

I can personally relate to almost every topic dealt with in this book. And, the feeling of inadequacy is no exception. No doubt my apologetic feelings about my appearance in earlier years—because I wore glasses and was slightly plump—took its toll. My slightly below average ability in sports left me periodically on the sideline. And as a teen-ager, I felt somewhat set apart because of my beliefs.

I succeeded in many things, but for some reason those successes were often obscured by insecurities. So I often overcompensated. For example, by the time I went to junior college I knew I wanted to become a physician. Knowing that outstanding grades were a prime prerequisite for admission to medical school, I undertook my college work with one primary aim—to get good grades so I could get into medical school. If I learned something, that was secondary. I was fully aware that such a plan was not the ideal, but I was more aware of my final goal. And I studied hard—for grades. Getting only a couple hours of sleep some nights, I carefully picked each class and instructor. If it looked like I might not get the grade desired, I would drop the class early in the year so it wouldn't show up on my record. When the grades were in, I felt somewhat bitter and resentful towards the two instructors who had given me Bs because I had worked hard and I felt deserved more. Towards all the rest that were As, I felt slightly like I had cheated the system and didn't quite deserve the high grade-point average with which I graduated.

Years have passed since those pre-med days and though inadequacies still creep in that must be dealt with, the Lord has taught me many things. It's beginning to dawn on me the tremendous implications of the completed work of Christ for me *personally*. His work *for* and *in* me does not depend upon my doing anything except believing it to be an accomplished fact. Realizing that I am "complete in Christ" (*see* Colossians 2:10 KJV) is helping abolish all insecurities and inadequacies. What also has been meaningful to me recently is to see how beautifully God lines up our abilities, interests, and opportunities to fulfill His will in our lives.

What is the solution to inadequacy, inferiority, insecurities, and feelings of total worthlessness? First and foremost we must start with God. Colossians 2:10 KJV says, ". . . ye are complete in him. . . ." Too often we human beings instinctively feel that God can't love us and truly accept us unless He finds something good in us. This is a problem whether we have initially accepted Christ as our provision for sin or not. We tend to perpetually slip back into the rut of thinking we must earn God's favor to have worth in His sight. The Pharisees were told in John 6 that *believing* is the work of God. Galatians 3:10 says that if a person relies on the work of the law he is under the curse. This may be diagramed as follows:

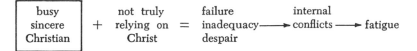

Eugenia Price states in *Woman to Woman* that in coming to Christ she became aware to be human is to be inadequate and adequacy only comes through Christ. 2 Corinthians 3:5, 6 says, "Not that we are sufficient of ourselves to claim anything as coming from us; our sufficiency is from God, who has qualified us. . . ." Christ then gives us worth. In fact, the value Christ placed upon human beings was enough to take Him to a cruel and undesired cross to redeem and ransom us. We are of value to the Creator of the universe, totally unrelated to any activity we accomplish. This is basic to the entire concept of God's grace. As we are obedient to God and He enables us to truly appreciate and accept these factors, we will gradually lose any sense of worthlessness or inadequacy. God loves me just the way I am.

The second step in solving the problem of inadequacy is to commit our life and work to God. If we don't do this, our activities will be at odds with God and feelings of failure will be understandable. Even if we have some successful pursuits, we realize down underneath that our works will end up as wood, hay, and stubble (see 1 Corinthians 3:10–15). "Commit your work to the Lord, and your plans will be established" (Proverbs 16:3). If we fail to do this, we are doomed before we start. Defeat, discouragement, depression, and fatigue lurk around the corner. We will either excuse ourselves or pursue our plans with frantic self-striving and self-effort. Either of these will bring further destruction and lead us away from God, His work for us, and His "promised rest." This in turn will lead us to internal conflict and weariness.

To truly commit our life and work to God there must even be a measure of disassociation from the work that we do. It is God's work. If the work goes well, we are to say, "We are unworthy servants," we have done just what God has wanted us to do (see Luke 17:10). On the other hand, if the work is God's and it seemingly totally fails from the human point of view, we must be able to say and mean that it is His work, He knows, He understands, even though we may not. Our value must remain in His love and grace toward us and the knowledge that He has accepted us just the way we are. We have no right to tell the potter how beautiful a vessel He should make out of the clay. We must be able to look around us and see our effort in shambles without condemning ourselves, if we have committed it all to Him. A pastor or church leader *must be able* to see his work entirely burned to the ground with no apparent results and still be able to trust it all to God.

This, admittedly, is a difficult task for any of us, but God can give grace. Job saw everything taken away from him and was ill on top of it all, but he was careful not to become bitter, blame others or God. God had His purpose which is seldom apparent at the moment of trial. Our value, then, is based upon our position in Christ and His love to us apart from works performed. Our business is to remain in fellowship with Him. It is His business what He wants to do through us.

If Christ had not had the eternal perspective, He would have had plenty of reason to be utterly discouraged and to feel a failure. Instead, He was able to say, ". . . I do always those things that please him" (John 8:29 KJV). That was the crux of His success. *The only thing which must matter in our lives is that we are doing what pleases Christ at this moment in time.* Then we can realize that our sufficiency is in Christ who provides the plus factor in life. The equation for adequacy is as follows:

$$\text{I} \quad + \quad \text{CHRIST} \quad = \quad \text{Adequacy for any job He ordains}$$

A few people are unwilling to take their eyes off themselves and their works and so, understandably, they feel worthless until they become willing to look beyond themselves to the plus factor in the equation—Christ.

The third step in resolving feelings of inadequacy is to truly accept ourselves, our abilities, our past. It is a fact that our innate abilities, achievement record, and opportunities both past and present tend to affect our view of ourselves. Sometimes our parents and our early environment may not have been as conducive to healthy self-acceptance as they might have been. However, bitterness and resentment, whether they are directed to God for our lack of innate abilities or to our parents or environment for lost opportunities, will only accentuate the problem. *God accepts us as we are. We must be willing to* give up any hostility toward God and others and *accept ourselves as we are. We must be willing to accept our past and the people that helped form it,* or our growth will be stymied the rest of our lives.

Some people actually condition themselves to fail. They do not feel worthy of success. The reason for this, I believe, lies primarily in not committing our life and works to God or an unwillingness to accept ourselves, our abilities, and our past, as they are and go on. If you are mad at God or your parents because of your inadequacies, you may unconsciously try and prove your point by *being* inadequate.

The fourth step in resolving our inadequacies is to realize that God has a plan and purpose for each life. I am a unique, special person to God. So are you. He has made only one of me, I am precious in His eyes, and He has created me for a purpose (more will be said about this in chapter 20). In John 15:16, Christ says, "I chose you." He has not only chosen us, but He has chosen the work that He wants us to do. Our responsibility is to follow His will in our life which is the road to adequacy in the human and finite as well as the eternal perspective. Living in His will, we will never be a misfit in any job, because the jobs will be chosen with His help. As we grow, He will line up our abilities, interests, and opportunities with His will for our lives.

The fifth step in growth from the feeling of inadequacy to adequacy is the realization that God wants you to succeed. He almost seemed upset at Moses for not believing he could succeed. It was said of David, "You will do many things and will succeed in them" (1 Samuel 26:25). Genesis 39:2 says, "The Lord was with Joseph, and he became a successful man. . . ." Paul the Apostle was a confident man, not in himself, because he had seen the fallacy of such, but in God and His ultimate plan for the universe and Paul's life in particular. So it isn't just a self-confident person we are talking about, but in reality a *God-confident person,* programmed for inevitable success in God's terms. It is through God, it is by God-given abilities, it is as

God directs, and the results are committed to His hand. Therefore a Christian should be characterized as realistic, confident, and from God's perspective, successful.

The sixth step in finding adequacy is the realization that we have only *one* Judge—God. We live in a highly competitive, judgmental society, often standing ready to criticize us at any opportunity. Everyone's standard for us is slightly different, making it impossible to measure up to all their expectations. The people with whom we rub shoulders are or may be more capable in some areas of their lives than we are in ours. But if we compare ourselves with them or allow their expectations for us to be our standard, we will come out on the short end. 2 Corinthians 10:12 KJV reminds us, "For we dare not make ourselves of the number, or compare ourselves with some that commend themselves; but they, measuring themselves by themselves, and comparing themselves among themselves, are not wise." God advises us ". . . not to think of himself more highly than he ought to think, but to think with sober judgment . . ." (Romans 12:3). We should honestly and realistically evaluate ourselves and compare this evaluation only with God's standard for our life.

Seventh on the list of solutions is to fulfill our rightful responsibilities. A student who neglects studying has an appropriate basis for feeling inadequate and insecure during final exams. As humans we all occasionally fail in meeting legitimate responsibilities. If we do this we must quickly admit it to ourselves, God, and, not infrequently, others. Then we must rectify it appropriately and go on.

The eighth point to remember is that life should be an exciting series of successful steps. Each new step should be slightly more difficult than the former. If what we have done is not challenging enough, we will lose interest in life and fatigue will set in. On the other hand, if we have been irresponsible or the tasks are beyond our reach—failure results. A series of such failures will leave its deep scars. Therefore under God's guidance, we should pace ourselves with jobs that are both challenging and yet within our reach so that we have a series of increasingly more important successes behind us.

Some people have a hard time seeing any successes in their lives. All they can see are the failures. If this is your problem, get out a piece of paper and list all the successes in your entire life. Include your abilities, strong points, and God-given gifts. If you have trouble doing this, ask another person to help you evaluate your capabilities.

The ninth point to remember in conquering inadequacies is that from a human perspective we will all occasionally seem to fail. As we look at individuals in the Scriptures, we find that if followed long enough they all seem to occasionally fail from the finite-human perspective. After his personal visit with God, Moses was convinced that he had failed in his leadership of the children of Israel. Elijah, who was God's prophet and upon whom God's blessing rested, was convinced he had failed. The Apostle Paul felt discouraged at moments when those about him seemed unfaithful. Even Christ Himself might have considered Himself a failure on many counts. He was despised and rejected by the majority. The Jewish nation to whom He came almost totally repudiated Him. Many people wanted only to use Him. He had at one time at least seventy disciples and when things got slightly rough he was left with twelve, and one of these was a traitor. At His deepest hour of need, all His disciples left Him and His most vehement follower denied Him three times. Even after His Resurrection, His disciples had to have proof, indicating their unbelief.

We must be willing to accept the fact that we are finite humans with limitations. However, through our eternal and absolutely perfect God, we can realize adequacy. In 2 Corinthians 12:9 KJV, Christ said to Paul, "My grace is sufficient for thee: for my strength is made perfect in weakness."

DISCUSSION QUESTIONS

*1) Do you often feel inadequate, insecure, inferior, or worthless?
*2) List the areas where you feel inadequate and the reasons for that feeling.
 3) List your strong points and successful past accomplishments.

4) Why might a person generally feel inadequate regarding his entire self and activities?

5) Do you agree with the eternal-absolute perspective and that on this basis we are all inadequate?

*6) Do you feel God loves you and you are truly of worth to Him regardless of any work you do?

7) Is there any place for a Christian to gain a sense of worth from what he does for Christ?

8) Should a Christian ever feel inadequate or worthless?

9) Do you agree with the equation:

$$\text{I} \quad + \quad \text{CHRIST} \quad = \quad \text{Adequacy for any job}$$
$$\text{He ordains}$$

10) How have you dealt with inadequacy?

11) Evaluate the insecurities or inadequacies of the following individuals and how they affected their lives:

a. Moses: Exodus 3:11; 4:1, 10–16; 32

b. Saul: 1 Samuel 15:17–24

c. Paul: Galatians 4:13, 14

8

BITTERNESS AND RESENTMENT

A young woman employee at the office where I practice came to me one day suffering from severe anxiety, fatigue, insomnia, and depression. She was an attractive girl in her early twenties and had always seemed happy and cheerful although she was not a Christian. Recently, however, she had married and after a few months of marriage her husband left her. She was now pregnant and stranded without financial resources.

She came to see me several times and each time the theme of her conversation was the same. She was filled with extreme bitterness and resentment toward her husband. I remember thinking many times, if she does not accept Christ and give up her resentment she certainly will have a life of bitterness and possibly will need prolonged psychiatric help. She was so depressed, in fact, that I decided if she did not respond after a few talks I would have to insist on psychiatric help, despite her limited finances.

Then one day in our living room, after listening to more of her bitterness, I said bluntly but kindly, "If you do not accept Christ and give up this resentment and bitterness, you are going to become a witch." We were both stunned by the directness of my words, but she admitted her bitterness, accepted Christ, and gave up her bitter feelings. The change in her was soon apparent to everyone who knew her. And fatigue was no longer a problem. Her abundant new life has had its struggles, but she remains a beautiful, joyful Christian.

Life is full of joys and sorrows, successes and failures, delights and disappointments. With so many seeming injustices beyond our control, we all have plenty of opportunities to develop bitterness and resentment. Other people most commonly incite our resentments, but in our computerized age there is no end to the causative factors. Husband may resent wife, children parents, youth the establishment, middle-aged people the changes of the youth, senior citizens inflation, the worker his employer, the taxpayer his government. In fact, resentment can develop against anything with which we come in contact, including inanimate objects like a computer or a car.

We are particularly vulnerable when a person or group of people has authority over us. Keith Miller, in *Habitation of Dragons,* notes that many ministers have to deal with the problem of resentment toward their parishioners. Forty percent of the people in an active, growing evangelical church said, on an anonymous questionnaire, that they too, were often bitter or resentful. Not infrequently, the resentment is really toward God, whether conscious or unconscious, for not giving us all we "deserve" or allowing "this" to happen to us.

I see bitterness and resentment overflowing from patients almost daily. And I am especially impressed with the frequent relationship of resentment and bitterness to depression. As with all unresolved internal conflicts, resentment may also rapidly lead to anxiety, fatigue, and psychosomatic illness.

Bitterness means a sharp disagreeable taste, discomfort, or pain. Resentment means a feeling of being injured or offended. Literally it means to sense or feel again. Many people knowingly harbor resentment and are acutely aware of a hostile, angry feeling springing up from within. This feeling may even cause their heart to speed up, moisture to appear on their brow and hands— their entire fight or flight mechanism may go into action with its resultant use of precious energy. But for some, bitterness and resentment are deeply repressed. The only manifestation may be that when a person or event periodically crosses their mind they feel slightly hurt, disappointed, neglected, or some other negative reaction.

Other times the bitterness is so repressed that we are not even aware of it. A minister once told me that he had been totally unaware for years of his resentment and hostility (though it was at times apparent to others), and that recently he went down to his father's grave and got rid of a "bellyful of resentments." Now he feels free and joyful. He previously suffered from severe fatigue but now reports he has at least three times the energy he used to have.

Most people for whom bitterness is a major problem tend to be "injustice-collectors." They frequently feel that they get the short end of the stick and actually unconsciously collect injustices. On the other hand, a single event which results in resentment and bitterness can alter the entire course of a person's life, such as the girl mentioned at the beginning of this chapter whose husband left her.

Bitterness and resentment usually are the result of some anger-producing situation that either should not have occurred in the first place or that was handled improperly. Anger often occurs when some basic need or "right" of ours has been jeopardized. We have been frustrated, hurt, disappointed, misunderstood, falsely accused, rejected, threatened, or made to feel jealous. Responding in anger to such situations is usually wrong. The basic problem should be dealt with *before* it produces anger, bitterness, and resentment. Colossians 3:8 and Ephesians 4:31 tell us to put anger from such causes out of our lives.

However, this does not mean that we should never get angry or that anger is always wrong. Sometimes anger is not sin. This is important to understand to avoid false guilt. Proverbs 16:32 and Ecclesiastes 7:9 warn us, however, to be slow to anger. Psalms 4:4 warns us that we must be careful not to slip into sin when angry. Ephesians 4:26, 27 NEB says, "If you are angry, do not let anger lead you into sin; do not let sunset find you still nursing it; leave no loop-hole for the devil."

The person who says he never gets angry either is not standing for anything worthwhile or, more likely, he is totally unaware of the presence of anger within him. The important thing is that anger be handled appropriately and as quickly as possible. If it recurs too often or persists, it certainly is sin and may actually stem from a hidden cause totally unrelated to the event we think makes us angry.

Anger-producing situations can be handled in two ways. Sometimes they require appropriate ACTION such as the time Christ cast out the money changers for defiling God's house and making it more difficult for people to come to God. To do less than this would be to shun standing for an important principle at a crucial moment.

However, when only self or ego is at stake in the situation, the proper action may be to totally ACCEPT and forgive. For example, Mark (chapter 5) tells us that a large gathering of people laughed at Christ for stating that Jairus's daughter was only asleep and not dead. After Christ raised her up, He could easily have made an issue of it and vindicated Himself, but He did not do so. Most of us would have marched the resurrected girl into the presence of the scorning crowd and in essence said, "See, I told you so." But Christ told the parents to keep it quiet while He inconspicuously left. If in such situations we do not totally accept and forgive, bitterness and resentment will enter in, which is never of God. This, says Hebrews 12:15, can grow like a cancer affecting all segments of our lives and many around us—even an entire church.

The key to dealing with anger is a willingness to forgive. Matthew 6:15 AMPLIFIED says, "But if you do not forgive others their trespasses—their reckless and wilful sins, leaving them, letting them go and giving up resentment—neither will your Father forgive you your trespasses." Often we are willing to forgive others if something they did was an accident. For example, if a man is driving down the street within the speed limit and hits your child who has darted out in front of him, it is not so hard to forgive him. However, suppose a teen-ager drives by at an excessive speed day after day and you warn him to slow down, then one day he hits your child—your willingness to forgive may be severely tested. If you do not forgive him, despite the difficulty of it, resentment will seep in and plague you from then on. We *must* forgive even another's "reckless and wilful sins."

Think how many times God forgives us. We all make mistakes day after day and God always forgives and allows us to go on. As humans, however, often we are not as ready to forgive others and allow them to go on. Sometimes we see a Christian leader and we know he has done something which seems to be outside of God's will; then we wonder why God uses him later. We sometimes forget that he may have dealt with this before God and heard God say, "Go on." Certainly God has used men such as David after they have committed serious sins.

While writing these pages, one morning a gentleman came to my office and served me with a subpoena for a court case involving one of my patients. Inwardly, I became angry and hostile. Most of this probably did not show, but I am sure some of it did. It upset the entire day for me as I reasoned, "Why should I be served with that subpoena? I had nothing to do with this patient at the time of his automobile accident. And, after all, there were many physicians who cared for him about the time of his accident. The trial could go on for days, upsetting my schedule. Why didn't the attorney subpoena the other physicians?"

And so my anger developed into bitterness and resentment. My pride was hurt because the attorney did not do me the courtesy of calling and explaining ahead of time. I tossed and turned for two nights, with resultant fatigue the next day, before I was willing to give up my resentment and before God say, "Lord what is Your purpose in this? Since I absolutely have no choice, You obviously must have a purpose and a big plan." With difficulty I yielded my will to His and said, "Lord, show me that plan, whatever it is." I thought maybe God wanted me to lead someone to Christ. Weeks later I received a phone call saying the case had been settled out of court and I could forget about the subpoena.

Now as I look back, my initial reaction looks so silly and insignificant, but at the time it didn't seem that way. I never did figure out what the "great plan" was except to test my yieldedness to Him, to people, and to circumstances.

The following two charts summarize the results of anger-producing situations which are handled inappropriately and appropriately.

INAPPROPRIATELY HANDLING ANGER

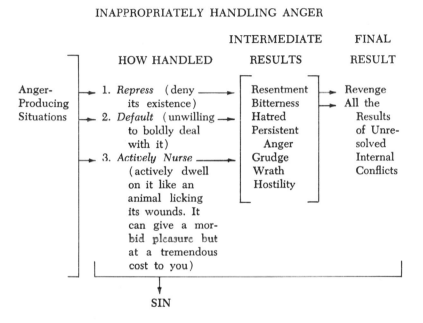

SIN

APPROPRIATELY HANDLING ANGER

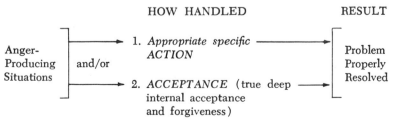

We must be willing to either act or accept; God will direct which course He requires of us. To act when we should accept is sin and to accept when we should act is sin. Some problems may require areas where action must be taken and other areas where acceptance is necessary.

We have discussed the relationship of anger to resentment and bitterness. Now let's look at some specific ways we can deal with resentment.

First, a proper walk with Christ is absolutely necessary. Many irritations and problems would never develop in the first place if your heart is right with God and your fellowman. On my desk I have a little reminder which says, "If things go wrong and you haven't spent sufficient time with the Creator of the universe, don't waste a lot of time looking for an explanation." This doesn't mean that other things can't be the cause. However, if another cause is not readily apparent and the channel is not wide open to God, the odds are very high that that is the underlying problem.

Second, there are times when we should avoid certain conflict-producing situations that may lead to problems which will produce little benefit to anyone. However, we must be careful not to use this as a "cop-out" when we should directly face and deal with a problem area if an important issue or lives are at stake.

Third, when you feel yourself becoming angry, bitter, or resentful, evaluate *why*. What is the basic cause? Dealing with superficial points of contention that are not the real underlying issue often only confuses the issues. Look below the surface. The first year of our marriage was the most difficult and punctuated with some emotion-filled arguments. We sometimes would argue around in a circle occasionally arguing over what started the argument. We were dealing only with superficial issues, and communicating on that level alone only made the matter worse.

Getting back to the basic cause of anger—occasionally the anger may be briefly justified. If that is the case don't condemn yourself as sinning. If, on the other hand, the anger persists and especially if bitterness or resentment are present, sin is involved on your part. If it is clear that you are entirely wrong, quickly go on to the next step—asking God's forgiveness.

However, the issues of life are seldom all black or all white. Especially in this area of bitterness and resentment there are usually shades of gray. Each person has his areas of right and wrong. One need not—should not—either whitewash or justify in appropriately another person when giving up resentments. If another person has a large or small part of the responsibility, that's his problem. Ours is to carefully delineate what part is our fault and responsibility, whether it is 5 percent or 95 percent, and to appropriately deal with it.

A practical suggestion along this line is to take a piece of paper and divide it into quarters. List areas where the other person was right and wrong and where you have been right and wrong. Also it is sometimes helpful to include factors in the other person's present and past life which may have been a contributing factor in how he acted. But be careful not to linger at this step too long. In the final analysis you must accept *full* responsibility for *any* aspects for which you *may* be responsible. You must then deal with your part of the responsibility, regardless of how he handles his part of the responsibility. It is often not our prerogative to show the other person his responsibility. Our aim should be to have a conscience void of offense toward every man, group, organization, and God (*see* Acts 24:16). We must forgive and have a clear conscience toward others even if they are unwilling to do the same toward us.

Fourth, we must ask God to forgive us for our sin in this matter. He will give us the gift of His forgiveness (*see* 1 John 1:9) and also remove our stony heart and give us a loving attitude (*see* Ezekiel 36:26, 27). In order to receive the gift of His forgiveness in a matter like this, we must be willing to make it right with the person involved (*see* Matthew 5:23, 24) as elaborated in step five below. The person who says, "I am willing to ask God's forgiveness but I will never ask so-and-so to forgive me" in effect blocks his receiving God's forgiveness.

Fifth, when confronted with an anger-producing situation in

which resentment can develop, we must be willing, without vindication, to deal with the situation and our feelings any way God directs—to forgive, to confess, to pay restitution, to accept, to forget, or to take any other specific course of action. We must prayerfully seek God's direction with complete openness and willingness to obey. Sometimes immediate or fairly quick action is indicated and other times it is wise to wait until emotions cool. Generally, God will direct us to take some SPECIFIC ACTION which may be as simple as admitting to someone we are angry or to totally ACCEPT the person and/or situation without any bitterness or resentment.

We must also be willing to deliberately not nurse our wounds with further thoughts of the issue. Not infrequently people say they will forgive but they "can't forget." On the surface this sounds good and legitimate. After all, they *did* forgive the person. And since we are all creatures with memories and have no way of obliterating something from our minds, the person who can't forget is seemingly merely making a statement of fact.

It is true that wounds leave permanent scars and some things are never exactly the same after an injustice has occurred. However, in every situation with which I have been familiar, the person emphasizing that he can't forget in reality has never truly forgiven or has been unwilling to do all in his power to forget. Neither of these just happen. Forgiving and attempting to forget are both a matter of the will. They both take effort.

Several years ago, I learned that to completely forgive was not enough. I also had to be willing to purposefully forget. The problem started when I was extremely busy for several months with my practice and other commitments. With the pressure of time, deeper communication with my dear wife, Betty, was lost. My feelings of love for her did not change, but I robbed her of the time and effort necessary to reaffirm this to her. As the weeks passed, I sensed something was not right with our relationship, but I was tired, arriving home late and leaving home early. I hoped the problem was just me or if it were more than that, it would naturally be resolved when my schedule lightened in a couple of weeks, or we could then work through the problem. Little did I realize the magnitude of the problem to Betty and that she did not see the end in sight.

In consideration of my time and pressures, she did not want to add to them some seemingly small problems that had occurred weeks prior. But now the problems had grown so that a solution did not seem forthcoming. In desperation she made an appointment with a friend who is a marriage counselor and left a note on my desk informing me of her action. When I found the note I was crushed and angry. I try so hard to be able to talk things over with people, but I had failed at home. How could I share Christ with others and be a leader if my relationship with my wife was not as it should be? I did not want to be a hypocrite. I am sure that the fear of what people might think was a factor also.

That night we talked and really communicated for the first time in many months. I assured her of my love and concern and that I was willing to stop every last one of the numerous committees and projects with which I was involved to make our marriage what it should be. I forgave her for making the appointment that affected both of our lives so deeply without first at least discussing it with me. However, despite making restitution and forgiving her, I repeatedly thought about the act that made me inwardly furious. In fact, I lay awake all that night thinking about it. (Fortunately this has never happened before or since.) I thought about it every free minute the next day and well into the next night. Finally I realized what was happening. I had forgiven, but I had also allowed myself to continue thinking about the incident. A morbid pleasure was gained from licking my open emotional wounds, but I could sense I was paying dearly for it. Because of the emotional involvement, I could feel the increase of adrenalin in my system and the sleepless night was not helping me either.

I promised God then and there that I would be willing to forget and would not allow myself to continue thinking about the incident. I endeavored to fill my mind with good, positive thoughts. Whenever I would momentarily think about my hurt feelings I stopped and forced myself to think about something positive. In a few days the crest was passed and it became much less a problem to discipline my mind. Now it is no longer an emotionally laden area. The initial problem was quickly dealt with, but had I not been willing to forget, the latter problem could have been far more detrimental than the precipitating event.

Sixth, we should ask Christ to fill us with the purifying Holy Spirit. We then must be willing to actively fill our minds and hearts with wholesome, positive thoughts including a joyful attitude, gratefulness, and rejoicing in Christ. This may take some effort, but true rejoicing in Christ inevitably displaces resentments. The author of Hebrews likens this to giving a sacrifice to God: "By him therefore let us offer the sacrifice of praise to God continually, that is, the fruit of our lips, giving thanks to his name" (Hebrews 13:15 kjv). 1 Corinthians 5:6, 8 refers to it as celebrating. Rejoicing, we must then move on in the job God has for us to do.

Each step suggested above is vitally important. Neglecting one can totally nullify a proper relationship with God, man, and ourselves. Omitting step five can produce a phony relationship with a mask. A willingness to do steps one through five, but not step six can leave you discouraged, introspective, and disappointed with yourself and others.

I am reminded of my brother, Dr. Paul Carlson, who was killed by the rebel forces in Kisangani, Zaire (formerly Stanleyville, Congo), in 1964. Leaving behind a good practice and the comforts of America, he went to a remote corner of Africa to minister to those needy individuals without a physician. He was loved by his people but then was captured, falsely accused, beaten, resented, hated, and ultimately killed by the rebels at thirty-eight years of age. Despite this, his great concern was for his family and that "through this we might see revival in our churches in Ubangi, in the hearts of all of us, and our Congolese brothers, too." His last written entry in his New Testament (the

night before his death) was, "Peace." He told a fellow prisoner
that he had no hostility against his captors and that if God
wanted him to return to Africa as a missionary, he would.

Remember, too, that the perfect Son of God came voluntarily
to this earth for you and me, was rejected by His own people,
ridiculed, beaten, and killed on a painful cross. Yet He bore all
this without resentment or bitterness. Such knowledge should
help resolve our petty grudges.

DISCUSSION QUESTIONS

*1) Do you feel you deserve more out of life than you are getting?
 2) Is there anything in life you can't accept? Should the word
    can't be changed to *won't*?
*3) Are you often bitter or resentful?
*4) What things do you commonly resent? List.
 5) Is there ever a time when anger, bitterness, or resentment are
    appropriate? Give examples.
 6) Do you think a person can carry a "chip on the shoulder" and
    not be aware of it?
 7) If a reckless driver killed your child should you (a) take him
    to court for his act (b) be angry, bitter, and resentful (c) both
    (d) neither? Explain.
 8) Should we forgive if the other person is not willing to?
 9) Should we ever go to a person and admit that we have been
    wrong in an effort to get him to admit that he has also been
    wrong?
10) Do you agree with the author that most people who say they
    can't forget really are just unwilling to forget?
11) How does our forgetting compare with the way Christ forgives
    our sin?
12) What is the difference between suppressing and repressing
    anger or resentment? Is either action appropriate?
13) In what specific ways do you handle resentments when they
    crop up?
14) If bitterness and resentment are so damaging, why do people
    nurse them? Can a person be a Christian and also be bitter?
    Can a person truly experience God's forgiveness and be bitter?

9

PAST AND FUTURE

I see many individuals, especially our dear senior citizens, who persist in living in the past. Week after week, month after month, they relive the past including its regrets, the things they would change, and also its pleasant moments. Often this leads to insomnia and depression. They are readily willing to admit they cannot change the past, but they are unwilling to make a serious effort to live in the present.

There is nothing wrong with learning and occasionally thinking about pleasant memories from the past; but to live in the past (with our minds frequently reliving what has happened) is, I think, sin. The Apostle Paul exhorts us to forget those things which are behind (*see* Philippians 3:13).

Why do we live in the past? First of all, I think it is because we are not willing to live in the present, with its new demands, involvements, issues, and battles to be faced. Living in the present requires positive pursuits of the mind and life. It takes work.

Or perhaps it is because we want to recapture and relive the pleasant memories of the past. Sometimes these memories are but an illusion, as suggested in Ecclesiastes 7:10, "Say not, 'Why

94

were the former days better than these?' For it is not from wisdom that you ask this." If we live in the past, we are actually wasting the present, which can result in personal loss and internal conflict.

Still others enjoy nursing the past of could-have-beens, reliving its regrets, disappointments, resentments, bitterness, and guilt. These acts may have been committed by the person or by someone else against him. Many resent what they think they have missed in the past.

It is a sin to live in such a state, a sin that can be passed on from one generation to another—often without the parent being aware of what he is doing. It permeates whole families. Only a bold, Christ-following person can break this unfortunate chain of events. Even if we know or think we have been wrong in the past it takes only moments to admit it to God. Some parents may need to go to their parents' graves, so to speak, to get rid of a "bellyful of resentments" before they can expect much of their children. To dwell on such thoughts is only to double or triple the sin.

When trouble started in the Congo, at first my brother Paul felt he should stay with his patients, despite the threats of the oncoming rebels. In a letter after his capture, he wrote, "I was wrong to try to stay, but I feel I put it all into God's hands and must leave it there." In this lies a lesson: whether you are in error or not, even if you don't know if you are in error, don't waste time speculating about it. Commit the situation to God and from that moment on follow His leading. Only then can you have peace and expect His name to be glorified.

One more comment to those who may be tempted to think they have wasted their lives and feel like "what's the use of changing now?" Perhaps you feel this way because you are elderly or have done "horrible" deeds in the past which left you feeling that those deeds prevent God's using you in the future. Or maybe you are a young person with an incurable illness and have only a short time to live. Regardless of your circumstances, remember the parable of the laborer in Matthew 20:1–16. Those who were idle all day but heeded God's call the last hour were rewarded equally with those who toiled all day. God can and will use you now if you will stop finding excuses.

It is pathetic to see a person refuse to start anew and follow Christ because he will have to admit he has been wrong for so long in the past. Saying you were wrong is such a small thing. But it leads to something great—the opportunity to start living joyously from that point on, positively influencing those about you. And with it comes the assurance that you are ready to face all eternity in a right relationship with God.

The future can also be a problem to many individuals, especially the younger generation. They often continually live in the future—imagining what life will be like when they finish school, get married, become established in a job, and have their financial problems basically resolved. On and on the illusion goes. If this type of thinking persists, one day it will dawn on the person that "his future" was a mirage. It is now past. Then instead of hope and optimism there comes discouragement, despair, guilt, and a tendency to live in the regrets of the past.

Those of us who are middle-aged sometimes tend to vacillate between the past and the future, or live in the next event in our life. *The person who has a meaningful tomorrow is busy with a meaningful today.*

This does not mean that we should never think ahead or plan for the future. Christ commended the wisdom of thinking ahead when planning a building, a tower, an engagement, and financial matters (*see* Luke 14:28–32 and Luke 16:1–9). We must use the brains God gave us to think and, within certain limits, to plan ahead. But at the same time we must be living in the present; our major energies, thoughts, desires, and actions must center around doing His will today.

Dr. William Oslo, a world-renowned physician at the turn of the century, used to speak about living in "day-tight compartments." By this he meant that most of one's energy and attention should be focused upon the tasks that lie within the present twenty-four-hour period. Even if today's road hits a rough spot, it is all the more reason to be careful to concentrate our efforts on living today and not to escape into yesterday or tomorrow.

Fellow prisoners of my brother talked about what they would do when they returned to the States. Paul felt he could not look forward to that but had to live day-to-day. He had one assurance though: "Where I go to from here I know not, only that it will be with Him."

An important element of the future about which people often worry is their health and death. When someone comes to me for a complete history and physical exam I ask him to fill out a health questionnaire. One question on the questionnaire is, "Do you have a fear or dread of death or the future?" At least 30 percent of the people answer yes to that question.

Existential psychiatrists believe that anxiety stems primarily from a fear of death. Yet any person who wants to can have eternal life and know beyond a shadow of any doubt that he is ready to meet God, has his sins forgiven and will be with God forever (see John 5:24; 1 John 5:11–13). At first glance one would think that a Christian should not be carrying this internal conflict of fear of the future and death. Unfortunately, a significant percentage do because they have not truly committed the past, present, and future—life, health, and death—to Him.

If only we could realize that worry not only does not help solve the problems we face, including our health, but so often it makes the problem much worse and increases the ultimate cost to us. Christ reminds us that by being anxious (see Matthew 6:25–34) we cannot add a moment to our life. Even the faithful Job (3:25) says, "For the thing that I fear comes upon me, and what I dread befalls me." Frequently the more anxious we become over the possibilities that a given undesirable event will occur, the greater the likelihood that it will in fact occur. All of this leads to internal conflict and fatigue.

The solution for living in the present involves learning to forget the past, trusting God for the future, and living for each day. We must be convinced of the fact that nothing can happen to us that is outside of His will for us except our own willful continuing in sin.

The formula is simple: ADMIT, COMMIT, FORGET. We should ADMIT that "cyclic thinking" (that is, thinking repeatedly about something long after it is likely to be beneficial) will not help and is actually very detrimental. We must ADMIT any sin, confess it to God and, if necessary, to the person we sinned against. We then must COMMIT it all to Him—the past, the future, the good, the mistakes, the questionable, the known, and the unknown. ADMITTING and COMMITTING should bring us to the place of ". . . FORGETTING those things which are behind, and reaching forth unto those things which are before" (Philippians 3:13 KJV). Philippians 4:6, 7 says, "Have no anxiety about anything, but in everything by prayer and supplication with thanksgiving let your requests be made known to God. And the peace of God, which passes all understanding, will keep your hearts and your minds in Christ Jesus."

Also, we must remember again that our minds and lives can't be a vacuum. We must actively follow God into the positive activities He has planned for us. Matthew 12:43–45 tells about the unclean spirit that left a man and because a better occupant was not found to replace the unclean spirit, the spirit took seven others and went back into the same individual. So it is with the past. We must be willing not only to deliberately forget it, but also to replace it with God's Word and current, meaningful activities ordained of God. *If God has given you breath, He has given you a purpose for this day.*

Matthew 6:25–34 NEB and TEV has some beautiful exhortations along this line such as, "Therefore I bid you put away anxious thoughts . . . Instead, give first place to his Kingdom and to what he requires, and he will provide you with all these other things. So do not be anxious about tomorrow; tomorrow will look after itself. Each day has troubles enough of its own." In other words, we have our hands full living for the present without wasting precious energy upon another segment of time for which we can do nothing at this moment. *In fact, today's neglect will be tomorrow's regret* and we will become weary in the process.

DISCUSSION QUESTIONS

*1) Do you often live in the past or future? Why?

*2) Do you have a fear or dread of death or the future?

*3) Do you worry about your health?

*4) Are you convinced that nothing can happen to you outside of God's will (except as a result of your own willful sin)?

*5) Do you deeply believe that God has a positive, useful, rewarding plan and purpose for your life that nothing (but yourself) can disrupt?

10

FINANCES AND POSSESSIONS

Chugging up a small hill the other day in my ten-year-old car, I noticed more than its share of pollution trailing out of the exhaust pipe. I deserve more than this, I thought. After all, I've been out of school seven years. I've worked hard. A man with my training deserves a better car than this.

It wasn't so much the threat of the car breaking down (although it had been towed away three days in succession for my wife), rather, I simply felt I *deserved* a better car. It's true we could easily borrow money for a new car. But with medical-school debts still unpaid and other demands, it didn't seem wise to go farther into debt at this time.

That same week a lady was talking to my wife, criticizing doctors in general for their "high" income and complaining about her own financial status. What she apparently failed to realize is that virtually everyone faces significant financial stress from time to time, at least from his own perspective. Although my salary is certainly adequate, it doesn't minimize the basic urge we all face to want more than we have. I know colleagues who make two and three times what I do and yet they live from paycheck to paycheck.

Recently a patient responded to a question regarding what he worries about by saying, "How to afford to simplify my job and life pattern." Many people can hardly live within their credit, let alone their income.

A recent article in the *Los Angeles Times* states that the average income adjusted for inflation in the United States for every man, woman, and child after taxes increased from $994 in 1911 to $2694 currently. The article further stated:

> American society is acquisitive. It is one of possession, competition, and change that generally is called progress. We are forever seeking new levels. Our appetites are insatiable. We live in a high pressure society. New images are placed before us by advertising. Desires are aroused. Competition is encouraged. Ambition is acclaimed, success admired and easy credit pays the way. If you remain unaware of the commercial world's methods you cannot deal with it on its own level. THE PERSON WHO REMAINS UNAWARE, WHO DOESN'T SET HIS OWN GOALS AND STANDARDS, LOSES HIS OPTIONS BY DEFAULT. HE WILL BE BUFFETED ABOUT. INSTEAD OF PURSUING A STRAIGHT COURSE, HE WILL REACT FRANTICALLY TO A MILLION STIMULI DIRECTED HIS WAY. HE WILL WONDER WHERE THE MONEY HAS GONE.

Undue concern about finances and possessions is just as great a problem for the middle class and rich as for the poor, for the average Christian as for the non-Christian. In one evangelical church 45 percent of those responding to a questionnaire said that personal or family finances occupied a prominent segment of time in their thought life. It is no wonder the Scriptures say, ". . . the love of money is the root of all evil" (1 Timothy 6:10 kjv). And the warning goes further to include all the things money can buy. 1 John 2:15 says, "Do not love the world or the things in the world. If anyone loves the world, love for the Father is not in him."

The person who increases his standard of living because he has failed to tune out the world and to tune in God will not only find that "He who loves money will not be satisfied with money; nor he who loves wealth, with gain" (Ecclesiates 5:10). He will also discover that STRIVING TO ACHIEVE THESE OVER-EXTENDED SELF-MADE GOALS WITH CARNAL ENERGY WILL PRODUCE WEARINESS AND ANXIETY OF BODY AND SOUL. This striving can become the cause of spiritual defeat.

I frequently see individuals whose financial problems, especially their debts or commitments, are creating tremendous internal turmoil resulting in anxiety, depression, resentment, bitterness, and fatigue. Occasionally, the magnitude of the problems helps push them into frank psychosis (nervous breakdown). And, surprising as it may seem, the problems are almost always of their own making.

Where does the problem start? I believe first of all it stems from the innate desire within all of us to have, hold, and accumulate. Our sense of worth, security, and importance is often wrongly tied to what we possess or the things we can do with our money.

A second reason is the thousands of subtle pressures around us which tend to influence us. Sometimes Christendom affects us as one more pressure instead of helping us with the basic problem. Christian leaders may resort to emotional pleas for the NEEDS of others, implying selfishness on our part if we don't give and give, in order to achieve their own selfish ends. Even though the Pharisees tithed, they didn't learn the more important basic principle of not loving money (see Luke 16:14). The great emphasis in the Bible about money and possessions is not tithing or the needs of other people, primarily. Rather, the emphasis is on the results of tenaciously wishing for, working for, and holding onto money and things, especially if it in any way comes between us and God. We cannot serve God and the world of possessions.

A third reason is that many people get into financial difficulties because of poor management. And, lastly, they often fail to trust and obey God in this vital area of their lives.

What is the solution? First, we must commit this entire area of our lives to God. Yielding every area of your life to God except the area of finances and possessions will lead to sorrow as you miss the true riches of life which God has for you. The rich young ruler (*see* Luke 18) apparently kept all of God's commandments (a remarkable feat) except that he was unwilling to yield his possessions. He missed the Kingdom of God, therefore, unless he later had a change of heart.

Remember Abraham. He had to be willing to yield his most precious possession, his son Isaac, without knowing whether God would return his son to him or not. Only when his yieldness was obvious did God return Isaac to him. Job lost all of his riches during the time of his trial. But later they were returned double ". . . when he had prayed for his [accusing] friends" (Job 42:10). God may or may not choose to take our possessions away from us. The important thing is that we, too, be willing to let Him do with them as He chooses.

Some people with small houses and few material possessions may think about and hold them more dearly than the rich. There is no relationship with how much we have or don't have and the magnitude of the problem of finances and possessions in our lives. The person with nothing may have a much bigger hang-up here than the person who is "rich." No matter what we have, the title must always rest in God's hand. Everything is safe when He holds the title, nothing is safe when we hold it. Our prime concern before money, possessions, and all other things must be to seek first the Kingdom of God and His will for our lives (*see* Matthew 6:19–34).

The second step is to realize that there is nothing wrong with money or things in and of themselves (*see* Titus 1:15). There are many examples in the Scriptures of rich people whose hearts were right with God. Jairus, the centurion, Lazarus, and St. Matthew are only a partial list, to say nothing of the patriarchs in the Old Testament. For the most part, God made no issue of what they owned as long as it did not hinder their relationship with Him. Zacchaeus was a "rich" chief tax collector who voluntarily gave half of his goods to the poor and offered to repay fourfold anyone he had defrauded (*see* Luke 19). He undoubtedly still was rich; but Christ, seeing his heart, verified its right relationship with God, and made no issue of his money or possessions.

The third step is a very practical one. There are a number of things you can do if there is just too much month left at the end of the paycheck. You can increase your earning ability through additional education or promotions. Overtime or an additional job has a place, occasionally, particularly under times of stress such as during educational years. But make very sure that the extra job is God's will, especially if you are continually wanting to earn more money. Careful planning and buying also have their place. The person who says only trust God and doesn't carefully plan his financial affairs is irresponsible.

Fourth, you must firmly decide that your standards are going to be different from the world's, including possibly many in the "Christian world." If your standards are going to be set under God's guidance, then you will have to tune the world out and God in. This doesn't just happen, it must be planned, executed, and repeatedly reevaluated.

Romans 12:2 PHILLIPS says, "Don't let the world around you squeeze you into its own mold, but let God remold your minds from within, so that you may prove in practice that the plan of God for you is good, meets all His demands, and moves toward the goal of true maturity." This means you must not only crucify the onslaught of pressures and standards from the world around you but also those from within. Do not compare yourselves with others, a tough job for us all. Your standard of living may have to be set several notches lower than your peers or friends.

Continually be on guard to avoid the high-pressure salesmanship techniques which can coax you into buying things you really do not need and may not even want. Even regarding pressures to give to the many worthy opportunities for the "Lord's work," we must get careful direction from God.

I particularly appreciate George Müller's comments (from Arthur T. Pierson's *George Müller of Bristol*) on the importance of systematic giving.

Only *fix even the smallest amount* you propose to give of your income, and give this regularly; and as God is pleased to increase your light and grace, and is pleased to prosper you more, so give more. If you neglect an *habitual giving, a regular giving, a giving from principle and upon scriptural ground* and leave it only to feeling and impulse, or to arousing circumstances, you will certainly be a loser.

In accordance with his suggestions, my wife and I sit down at the beginning of each year and before God carefully decide what percentage He would have us give during the coming year.

Fifth, you must be willing to ruthlessly follow through on God's direction regarding your finances and possessions. If you have certain weaknesses in the area of follow-through, identify them and take the necessary steps to avoid making serious mistakes. Many years ago, I determined under God's guidance to limit my practice so that I would have time to do many other things that I felt my life should include. Despite this resolve I became aware of the subtle tendency to allow my practice to increase for financial reasons, which, of course, decreased available time. To help me curb this, several years ago we determined to give four times our usual percentage to God's work if a certain base income was surpassed. This, along with Uncle Sam's cut, removed the incentive to work more hours for personal financial gain and thus helped me obtain my basic goals.

Finally, be assured that God, our loving heavenly Father, knows your needs and will meet them. When you turn your deep yearnings over to Him, He will refine them and give you what is consistent with His will and often what you really want. He may even choose to give you back something you earlier had to sacrifice. Paul said in Philippians 4:11–13, 19, ". . . I have learned, in whatever state I am, to be content, I know how to be abased, and I know how to abound; in any and all circumstances I have learned the secret of facing plenty and hunger, abundance and want. I can do all things in Him who strengthens me. . . . And my God will supply every need of yours according to his riches in glory in Christ Jesus."

"Keep your life free from love of money, and be content with what you have; for he has said, 'I will never fail you nor forsake you' " (Hebrews 13:5).

"There is great gain in godliness with contentment . . ." (1 Timothy 6:6–12).

"Take heed and beware of all covetousness; for a man's life does not consist in the abundance of his possessions" (Luke 12:15).

DISCUSSION QUESTIONS

°1) Are you satisfied with your material status? Should you be?

°2) Do your personal or family finances occupy a prominent segment of time in your thought life?

3) Do you agree that a Christian's standards regarding financial matters must be different from a non-Christian's? Explain. In what way are your standards different?

4) Do you think Christians ever try to "trust God" for needs that either were never His desire for them or in which they have failed in their responsibility in the matter? What are the long-term results of this?

5) Do you think churches (and sometimes other Christian organizations) are ever guilty of paying their pastors too little and creating tremendous internal conflict? What is the proper and improper place for "faith"?

6) In 1 Timothy 5:17, 18 LB it says: "Pastors who do their work well *should be paid well* and should be highly appreciated. . . ." In the TEV and NEB translations it goes so far as to say that Christian workers should receive *double pay* and *double stipend*. What are the beneficial results of paying Christian workers well? What are the detrimental results of underpaying them?

7) If finances and possessions are a problem is it because we aren't committed enough to God—or is it actually because we are too committed to money, things, ambitions, etc.?

11

THE HOME, SEX, AND MARRIAGE

I drive past our children's school to and from work and occasionally pass it during a recess or lunch hour. Usually I slow down and look for either one of those special kids I love so dearly. If I see one, I pause in appreciation for the child God has brought into my life.

On one particular day my eyes fell on Susan, who was then about six years old. A rough boy was pushing her around despite her seeming pleas for him to stop and her attempts to run away from him. I felt like a knife was being pierced through my heart. It wasn't that he was doing any serious physical harm to her, but obviously she was hurting emotionally. I was stunned as I stopped the car and debated whether to jump out of the car, run across the street, and yell at the bully from the fence, or go up to the gate and inside the grounds to alert the playground attendant of the problem. But within a moment, Susan had gotten away from him.

I sat there in the car a few minutes longer wondering whether to talk to the principal, but decided it probably wouldn't make much difference. Being "pushed around" at times is part of life for all of us. At times we can minimize it and not "ask for it," but we can never completely eliminate it. It is part and parcel of living in this often hostile, competitive, aggressive, self-seeking world. The important thing is that we have a SAFE PLACE to come home to. A place where we experience acceptance, communication, openness, times of fun, and the ability to love and be loved, free from manipulation. A SAFE PLACE will help replenish energy used during the day and refresh us for the next day of confrontation with the world. The person whose home is not a SAFE PLACE will often be weary before he walks out the door in the morning.

Conflict within the home creates conflict within the individual with all the inevitable results including fatigue. This not only includes conflict between husband and wife, but also between children. Unruly children not only wear on their parents, but on others around them. This reminds me of the businessman with an ulcer whom I was querying about possible stresses at work and in life. "Work's great," he told me. "It's at home where all the problems are."

How does one create a SAFE PLACE at home? Hundreds of books have been written on this subject from the vantage point of husband, wife, parent, and child. Obviously I cannot scratch the surface in one short chapter. However, I do want to point out that a troubled home may be the major cause for fatigue, anxiety, depression, or psychosomatic illness. If this is a problem area for you, ignoring it will only magnify the problem. Get appropriate help through books, a marriage counselor, your pastor, or some other qualified person. Applying the suggestions covered in this book will resolve most problems in the home.

One comment about the many voices giving advice on how to raise children. There are basically three approaches: the authoritarian, permissive, and various twists to the democratic approach. I personally lean toward a cross between the democratic and authoritarian methods. However, I really think the method is less important than the underlying motive behind the method. Do we really love, care, respect the rights of, and communicate with our children? Do we appreciate the God-given worth of the individual? And are we consistent? In my opinion these factors are more important than getting uptight about following a given approach.

As we personally grow in love we will find that "love can cover [cancel] a multitude of sins" (1 Peter 4:8 PHILLIPS). It means we must be willing to learn to work through our problems of living in close proximity with other human beings and not just "walk around" troubled areas. It means communicating on deeper and deeper levels as the years pass. This communication is the essence of a deep marital relationship. Dealing with problem areas must start with *you*. True love will permeate an entire household if it is kindled by a person who has no ulterior motives.

A successful marriage can never be a fifty-fifty deal. Our myopia (near-sightedness) will always fail to see many good things our mate has done while vividly seeing, remembering, and keeping score of the good things *we* have done. Thus, in any so-called fifty-fifty relationship, whether it is marriage or a business partnership, if you do not love and give beyond your share, you will continually weigh your mate's good and bad deeds. Invariably your mate will come out short. If you really want your marriage and your home (including children) to be a loving SAFE PLACE, readjust your thinking to a ninety-ninety deal. That is, you must be willing to gladly go at least 90 percent of the way in your marriage to give of yourself and your love. Isn't this, after all, the meaning of love? Remember, however, that true love never negates appropriately disciplining your children (*see* Proverbs 29:17; 13:24).

Just a comment regarding sex. Sex is a gift from God and in its proper place consummates the growing beautiful marriage relationship. In fact, it is often a good indication of how the person and the marriage are going. It is like an elevated temperature. If you are married and sex is not truly satisfying, something is wrong. In almost every situation it means there are significant conflicts within the marriage relationship or unresolved conflicts within at least one of the marriage partners. It may well be that these same internal conflicts are also causing fatigue or other inevitable results. How,ever, it should be added that a pleasurable sexual relationship does not always mean that all is going well with the marriage or individual.

What about the single person who deeply desires to find a SAFE PLACE in marriage. This is a perfectly normal desire, but like all other desires it must be given totally to God. Not to do so makes it difficult or impossible to find God's will, His plan, and His peace. Unyieldedness in this area may also actually interfere with finding a mate. God will compensate for these legitimate needs if marriage is not in His plan for you. Let me illustrate this point by telling you about a single woman I'll call Sandra. As with most single gals, she went through a period of several years wondering what the future held for her. Would she ever be married and have a family, which she greatly desired? These questions were punctuated with episodes when she was "very depressed, very tired, and very confused." The symptoms persisted until she honestly admitted her deeper feelings—her desire for marriage. She also realized that marriage was probably not in God's plan for her life. She committed all of these things honestly to Christ. Simultaneously facing herself, she gradually became aware of her own strengths, abilities, and gifts. She found a new interest and ability in unselfishly loving children and helping others in need. She associated with a church fellowship which allowed her the freedom to be herself and "do her own thing." Today Sandra has found a new purpose for life which has displaced the symptoms of fatigue, depression, and confusion. It is not that she never thinks of the future possibility of marriage or that this is never a problem to her. But she has basically dealt with the problem and God has given her fulfillment, satisfaction, and a purpose in life as she finds it.

When I was single I wasted hundreds of hours thinking and hoping for a meaningful marriage. Certainly God does not want us to enter lightly into this extremely important relationship. However, one must not live in the future in this regard either.

At one time there was a particular girl I thought must be God's choice for me. I spent scores of hours thinking about her and our future together until it became a form of covetousness and idol worship. Wanting to please God, I became convicted that I was living in the future, so I greatly decreased the amount of time spent thinking about her. However, I soon found that virtually every time I prayed I brought the same request about her to God. Then I became aware of the verses which state that the children of Israel ". . . lusted exceedingly in the wilderness. . . . And he gave them their request; but sent leanness into their soul" (Psalms 106:14, 15 KJV). This made me aware that prayer about this subject was another form of not committing the matter to God. I purposed to pray about it once more, then commit it completely to Him and not pray about it again until I felt so led by Him. The deceitfulness of our human hearts can even deceive us in what we pray for unless we are led by the Holy Spirit in all of these acts.

One more area deserves attention because it creates a tremendous amount of internal conflict, especially anxiety, in those who indulge in it. That area is illicit sex and the various forms of sexual perversion. Those who are trapped in adultery, fornication, homosexuality, and other forms of sexual perversion must see the sinfulness of your deeds (1 Corinthians 6:18, 20, Romans 1) and seek forgiveness and deliverance through the grace of God. You must also be willing to totally abandon such practice.

A graphic example of how this type of internal conflict can cause fatigue, anxiety, sin, and death is illustrated in 2 Samuel 13. David's son, Amnon, loved his sister to the point that he was "so tormented that he made himself ill." Dissipation of energy caused his friend to remark, "Why are you so haggard morning after morning?" Because he refused to curb his sexual passions, he not only was tired but sinned and, ultimately, it cost him his life.

DISCUSSION QUESTIONS

°1) Is your home an emotionally safe place? Is it safe for all members of your family?

*2) Do you "walk around" troubled areas in your marriage or are you able to openly discuss any area with your mate? What are the eventual results of walking around such areas? Do you walk around areas with your children? List the areas and why.

3) What do you think of the idea of marriage being a ninety-ninety deal? Is this practical?

4) Do you agree that a poor sexual relationship in marriage is usually an indication of unresolved internal conflict within one or both individuals? Are there exceptions?

5) Do you agree that we can actually covet in our prayers? Have you ever done this? Give examples.

12

RIGIDNESS, COMPULSIVENESS, AND LEGALISM

Another form of internal conflict producing fatigue is rigidity. A rigid person is one who is poured into a mold of his own making or one made by others. His life is constricted, inhibited in growth and expression. Literally, rigid means "to be stiff" and "to be right." It also means inflexible, unyielding, firm, or severe. The rigid person lacks teachability, pliability, openness of heart, mind, and ideas.

Rigidity is caused primarily by compulsive impulses from within or by legalistic requirements imposed from without. Both of these produce tremendous bondage, internal conflict, and fatigue.

A compulsive person tends to be formal, meticulous, perfectionistic, overly inhibited, self-doubting, and fastidious. He is often compelled by forces from within that he does not understand to perform activities which he would rather not undertake. This can vary from a very mild and sometimes good characteristic to the compulsive neurosis often characterized by the insistent hand-washer.

The person with compulsive tendencies finds it hard to relax, follows a literal obedience, has an exaggerated sensitivity, often is stubborn, and feels harassed by responsibility, though he is often a hard worker. He often will compulsively do unimportant things, forcing him to neglect the far more important responsibilities.

An example might be a compulsive housewife who prides herself in having everything just right. Then on a given evening, whether through poor planning, an accident, or unexpected interruptions, she has four hours of work to do and only two hours before the dinner guests arrive. If she cannot redefine her priorities and decide what can and must be done in the two hours, she is liable to be very frustrated and anxious. She may develop such a state of panic that she does not properly utilize the time she does have and may even ruin the evening for everyone involved.

As Charlie W. Shedd points out in *Time for All Things*, all of us face "divine interruptions" which can throw a monkey wrench into our plans if we are rigid and compulsive. Sometimes these divine interruptions are our greatest potential opportunities. We must be able, at a moment's notice, to reevaluate and place a new order on priorities. Without the right amount of flexibility, we will become shackled by our own lock and chain which produces weariness.

What are the causes for these uninvited internal impulses? I believe they often stem from repressed and unconscious bitterness, resentment, guilt, anxiety, or insecurity, which may have originated years earlier in the individual's life. To effectively deal with this compulsive behavior means that we must resolve the deep internal conflicts responsible for the behavior. (*See* chapters 5, 7, 8 in particular.)

Legalism results when rigidity is imposed primarily from *outside* oneself. It may be imposed by individuals, organizations, society, or doctrinal code. The compulsive individual is much more prone to become legalistic. Often it is hard to know if the rigidity actually started from within or was imposed from without. Legalism becomes a particular problem in all religions. Unfortunately, it is a problem in Christianity, too. The early church faced the problem of legalism almost immediately after its formation and we find that Paul adamantly crusaded against it. Individuals as well as large movements often quickly lose their spiritual fervor and freeze in a chilling mold of legalism.

Unfortunately, most rigid, legalistic individuals and groups fail to recognize it in their lives. Most Christians readily recognize the legalism of the Pharisees which included such minutiae as tithing of spices and traveling no more than six blocks on the Sabbath. However, we often fail to see the thousand-and-one ways in which legalism can creep into our own lives. If we define legalism in the Christian's life as any activity or service which ceases to be done primarily for Christ or because we are convinced He wants us to do it, it allows a more accurate measurement. It is the fulfilling of a law, code, set of activities, or what is expected of us instead of seeing the prime motivation— pleasing Christ in all that we do and think. It is performing religious acts and losing sight of the reason for doing them. In fact, frequently fulfilling our legalistic ritual becomes more important than the reason for which we initially undertook it. Legalism is not only doing the wrong thing—it may be doing the right thing for the wrong motive.

For example, is attending church twice on Sunday and at least once during the week legalism? Is supporting a program long after it's dead, giving to the Lord's work, or rigidly praying before each meal (as long as it's not just a snack) ever legalistic? Could having a Bible study or prayer group ever be included in this list? Is continuing as a Sunday-school teacher or board member ever legalistic? Do ministers ever stay in the ministry and missionaries on the mission field because of legalism? And while we are at it, what about one's own personal Bible study, prayer, and quiet time? In my opinion, all of these great activities *may* become totally legalistic. If you think my language is strong, consider what Paul had to say about it in Philippians 3:8. Or consider Christ's comments to the Pharisees in Matthew 23.

Several months after recovering from the exhaustion described in chapter 1, I joined the navy, feeling that this was God's will for my life. I was determined to live for Him in this new setting. However, the rigors of boot camp were strenuous with virtually every minute filled between the early reveille and late taps. I was able to spend time in prayer while marching or waiting in line, but some days I legitimately was unable to spend time in God's Word. And so, legalistically, I would spend time after taps in the bathroom reading God's Word, the only place where the lights were allowed. Unfortunately, most of these times it wasn't done because I wanted to spend time with God—I was too tired—it was because I felt I should adhere to a standard. Later aboard ship I used a personal checklist as a standard and tool to stimulate my obedience and growth. It eventually grew so that over fifteen areas were checked. Most were evaluated daily but a few several times a week. It included such items as time to bed, time to rise, witnessing, and length of quiet time. For a while I even checked that I sacrificed breakfast if I was negligent in getting in my early morning quiet time (*see* Job 23:12). Soon my life was so filled with religious "do's" that I added to my checklist reading of *Time* magazine in an effort to stay abreast of current events. This may well have been a necessary step in growth and undoubtedly I learned much from it. But unfortunately I didn't know how to keep it from becoming a self-imposed legalistic burden.

Even in recent years I have found it difficult to stay home at 11 A.M. Sunday morning and spend time in Bible study, prayer, and quiet meditation when I felt God wanted me to do this, instead of legalistically attending church. More recently I stopped a series of home Bible studies and found it again difficult to break the rigid mold. The fact that I am convinced that God was in them and they continued for seven years beneficially touching a number of lives didn't matter one iota. The fact was now that God was leading me out of this and to feel that I should continue them was not only legalism, but sin. The real problem was time and priorities. Some of us have a tendency to get so busy in religious "shoulds" that we don't have time to do the "shoulds" that God wants us to do. This is legalism. I hasten to add I am not decrying any of these, I am only trying to put them in their proper perspective.

Most of us evangelicals have it clear that we are not saved by works. We have it clear that the purpose of the law is to reveal sin (*see* Romans 3:20; 5:13). But we have failed in deeply realizing that we do not maintain God's favor by adhering to an external standard or legalistic code.

Whenever legalism creeps in, we become insensitive to God Himself. There is a tendency to either throw off all standards, which produces spiritual and moral anarchy, or to continually add to the standards until they become impossible to fulfill. We then become disillusioned and either give up or strive in carnal energy to work harder. Either way we come out on the short end, feeling guilty, tired, and depressed.

The burden of legalism is a tremendous one (*see* Matthew 23:4, Luke 11:46). Legalism leads to duty, fear of punishment, and an opinionated, hairsplitting, critical individual. This is in contrast to the life which should be characterized by love, liberty, and freedom. And remember that legalism results in God's name and work being "blasphemed," no matter how good and right the religious act may be (*see* Romans 2:17–24).

What are the causes that lead us into legalism? First of all, it may have its roots in the basic compulsive tendencies of an individual. If so, there may be some basic unresolved internal conflicts such as guilt, bitterness, resentment, anger at God or man, or insecurities which must be dealt with.

The second cause of legalism is an unwillingness to be truly spiritual. Legalism is what we manufacture when we aren't truly obedient to God. If one knows the truth and fails to do it, he is often led into bondage; however, if one learns the truth and truly does it, this leads to freedom. It is a lot easier *to do* than *to be*—that is, it is a lot easier to conform to an external code than to be the kind of person God wants us to be. God wants us *to be*. To conform to an external code is predictable. To be the kind of person God wants us to be is less predictable in terms of external acts. To only *do* is sin. For if we are not willing to allow God to change the inside as well as the out, we are holding back from God and putting on a mask.

The third cause for legalism is a misunderstanding of God's message to man. The doctrine of grace is not only that man cannot come to God on the basis of any of his good works (*see* Romans 3:27; 4:4, Galatians 3:10), but also as Christians our basis for continued acceptance by Him is completely dependent on what He has done for us. Satan and our unregenerated nature tend to constantly want to add to what God has already done. In fact, there tends to be a pseudospiritual feeling that the more one adds to God's requirements, the more spiritual he must be. This entirely misses the heart of the gospel. This new relationship excludes relying on action or being proud about what we have done (*see* Galatians 3:10, Romans 3:27). Instead of a relationship of duty with punishment and rewards, it is a relationship of obedience with liberty. John 8:36 says that if the Son liberates us we are free indeed.

Another way we misunderstand God's message to us is to follow the line of logic which states that every *word* in the Bible is inspired, therefore every *word* must be of equal importance to us. This type of thinking causes one to miss the relative importance of one portion of the Scriptures as compared to another. One can easily miss the very heart of God's message through this thinking. In essence, one can fail to see the forest because of the trees.

Let me explain. The Ten Commandments were all given by God, but sometimes one takes precedence over the application of another. They may, at times, seem to contradict each other. Christ knew that the Sabbath was instituted to facilitate man by setting aside a day so that he might be refreshed spiritually and physically. He therefore allowed His disciples to pick corn on the Sabbath day which violated the Pharisees' understanding of the Fourth Commandment (*see* Mark 2:23–28). Though they weren't aware of it, they ended up rejecting the First Commandment—and the most important one—loving God—in their legalistic effort to keep God's Fourth Commandment. Christ, in fact, commented to the Jews in Mark 7:9, "You have a fine way of rejecting the commandment of God, in order to keep your tradition!"

If one places the same value on all commands, rules, good acts, and worthy endeavors, before long confusion and an unbearable burden develops, producing fatigue. And in the process the wrong thing may get tossed out. God's will is dynamic (*see* chapter 17). We must see then that the message God would have us learn is that immediate and continual obedience to Christ is our highest aim. Christ summed it up to the Jewish leaders, " 'Love the Lord your God with all your heart, soul, and mind.' This is the first and greatest commandment. The second most important is similar: 'Love your neighbor as much as you love yourself.' All the other commandments and all the demands of the prophets stem from these two laws and are fulfilled if you obey them. Keep only these and you will find that you are obeying all the others" (Matthew 22:37–40 LB).

The fourth cause of legalism is people pleasing. Matthew 6:1 tells how the Pharisees observed the external legalistic code so they might be considered "spiritual." Galatians 2:12 and 6:12–14 indicate that the motivation is either a good showing or to avoid people's displeasure. Unfortunately, a lot of Christian service is being done to be seen by other men. More will be said about this in chapter 14.

The fifth cause of legalism is ego-gratification. The Books of Galatians and Romans tell how people boasted in their religious accomplishments (*see* Galatians 6:13).

The sixth reason for legalism is misinformed, naïve, or selfishly motivated leaders. Legalism is easier to teach. It is more predictable and controllable. It intuitively seems safer. External results are often quicker and more apparent. (*See* Acts 15:10; Galatians 1 and 2; and in this book, chapters 16, 17, and 18.)

How can we conquer legalism? First of all, one must be sure of his position in God. Sure of his salvation, sure that there is no unconfessed sin, or other unresolved internal conflicts for which God requires action. Paul's solution for legalism is summarized in Galatians 2:20 which says, "I have been crucified with Christ; it is no longer I who live, but Christ who lives in me; and the life I now live in the flesh I live by faith in the Son of God, who loved me and gave himself for me."

The second point in solving the problem of legalism is to understand what God's demands are. Romans 12:2 PHILLIPS says, "Don't let the world around you squeeze you into its own mold, but let God remold your minds from within. . . ." We must stop listening to the world about us—sometimes even the Christian world. Then we must listen to God through His Word and Holy Spirit. This takes time alone with God and His Word to get our signals straight (see Galatians 1:16–18). It can't be rushed without missing some important point (see chapter 22). There is also an element of simplicity in this relationship (see 2 Corinthians 11:3). Legalism is abolished by a responsive heart to God.

This leads me to the next point in solving the legality problem. In reality it is God's prime solution, i.e., His Holy Spirit or Counselor to direct our lives, actions, and thoughts moment by moment and from within. He is a sure cure for legalism. "Now the Lord is the Spirit, and where the Spirit of the Lord is, there is freedom" (2 Corinthians 3:17). "For all who are led by the Spirit of God are sons of God" (Romans 8:14). And in Galatians 5:18 it says: "But if you are led by the Spirit you are not under the law."

However, though the Holy Spirit is readily available to us, if we are not careful we can relegate Him to our benediction both literally and figuratively. That is, we may use His name when we say, "In the name of the Father, Son, and the Holy Spirit," and we may ask His blessing and concurrence on what we have already decided. Some people, in fact, are living essentially in an Old Testament experience, even though they are aware of and verbalize all three Persons of the Trinity. In reality they function as if bound to laws, traditions, and legalisms, with the result of bondage and fatigue. Others may be living comparable to the disciples' relationship when Christ walked on the earth. They left their all, but they were weak, fearful, defeated, and self-seeking. Christ told His disciples of a better way. That it was to their advantage that He leave so that the Counselor could come and He would guide them into all truth (see John 16:7-15).

Recently I was reading through Acts to reevaluate the frequency and emphasis on God the Father, Son, and Holy Spirit. I found that God and Christ were each referred to about three times as often as the Holy Spirit. Praise, glory, and worship were given to God and Christ whereas the emphasis regarding the Holy Spirit was more of acknowledging His function and authority (see John 16:13, 14). The Holy Spirit could not be ignored or neglected without great consequences, and on the other hand undue attention on the Holy Spirit and His manifestations for secondary gain was not tolerated (see Acts 8). To me there is a beautiful balance between equal praise and glory to God the Father and God the Son and recognition of the important role of the Holy Spirit in my life—to fill me with His divine presence and direct me in my moment-by-moment life, freeing me from the bonds and slavery of legalism.

The next point in solving the legalism problem is honesty. One would think this would not have to be mentioned. However, Paul says in Galatians 2:14 that certain Jews were not straightforward about the gospel. When one is bound in legalism, often there is an element of dishonesty (see Matthew 23:3) both to others and to oneself. The mask is a frequent accompaniment of legalism. There is a strong tendency to convey a greater degree of spirituality than actually exists. One then must be honest about himself, to deal with legalism in his life. (See chapter 6.)

The fifth point in helping to solve the widespread problem of legalism is to allow others their rightful freedom. The Pharisees and the early church (see the Gospels, Acts, Galatians) quickly taught others their legal hang-ups. We should learn this lesson and be very careful about imposing what God requires of us on another (see Acts 15).

The next point is that *we must stand firm in our freedom.* Galatians 5:1 says: "For freedom Christ has set us free; stand fast therefore, and do not submit again to a yoke of slavery."

Paul opposed the most prominent disciple over this issue (*see* Galatians 2:11). Christ's harshest words were against the Pharisees who were entangling others in their rigid codes. God wants us to have freedom (*see* Galatians 5:13). We may have to actively resist other Christians over this issue. (*See also* Colossians 2:16–23.)

The last point on solutions to legalism is to *keep a constant vigilance to avoid slipping back into legalism*. What was done out of obedience to Christ yesterday may be done out of legalism today. Paul was "astounded" that this happened so "quickly" to the zealous early Christians (*see* Galatians 1:6). And one "little" legalistic activity can soon entangle our entire life into one of bondage (*see* Galatians 5:7–9). *If we do not maintain our freedom, we will slip back into bondage.* Legalism is what sets in if there is no new growth and obedience in the Christian life.

My wife struggled with legalism for several years. Working for salvation was never her problem—she realized there was nothing she could do to merit it. However, she wanted to grow as a Christian, to be a "good Christian," so she worked hard at it— regular Bible study, prayer time, reaching out to others, and so on. If an internal problem ever surfaced, the usual remedy was "just study harder, and pray more." After some years of this, she says she was "emotionally and physically exhausted and spiritually empty."

At this point in her Christian growth, she realized she was trying to keep up with another person's standards of growth. In the process she was failing to realize the Holy Spirit's direction and prodding in her life. She then refocused her eyes from man to God. She became increasingly sensitive to the Holy Spirit, realizing He was the teacher and that she was responsible to God only. Leaving the security of legalism was at first a frightening experience, but she appreciated a new form of liberty, freedom, and energy not previously experienced. During this early phase of liberty she was faithful in her personal fellowship with God. But as time passed, this became less consistent, and when important Christians in her life misunderstood her liberty, she became somewhat resentful, gradually slipping into a phase devoid of both legality and liberty. She has subsequently found the balance which includes liberty, with obedience, responsibility, and a conscience void of offense toward God and man.

Let me hasten to add a word of warning. Here again Satan is the author of extremes. He is happy if we are bound in legalism or if we are loose in uncontrolled liberty, leading to license and irresponsibility. I am fully aware that by debunking legalism something which I have said can be taken out of context and be used for license. The possible results of reading this chapter are outlined in the figures below. In figure A one can remain in legalism and bondage which result in fatigue, and all the other internal conflicts including sin.

Figure A

Legalism and Bondage ———→ Legalism and Bondage (May change forms of legalism) ———→ (With resultant fatigue and other internal conflicts including sin)

Or one could swing the pendulum to the opposite extreme, and move from legalism and bondage to liberty without obedience or responsibility. This ultimately will lead to spiritual shipwreck with all that this implies. Figure B illustrates this course:

Figure B

Legalism and Bondage ———→ Liberty without Obedience ———→ Spiritual shipwreck

I prayerfully hope that you will follow the course in figure C. If you are in legalism and bondage now, that you will find liberty in and through Christ with obedience and a responsible life to Him. This will lead you to the abundant life with increased energy.

Figure C

Legalism ─────────────▶ Liberty ─────────────▶ Abundant life
   and   with   (with increased
Bondage   Obedience   energy)

What are the results of the liberated life free of legalism? How can one know he has not just drifted from legalism to license? The life that Christ has liberated and freed will have as its orientation—not others or their codes, or ourselves and what we want to do, but Christ and His wishes for our life. It will necessitate obedience and responsibility directed towards Him (*see* Romans 3:31). In some ways this standard is actually higher than the law (*see* Matthew 5:17–24). The Old Testament said "do not commit adultery." The New Testament not only says "do not commit adultery," but "do not have thoughts of adultery" (Matthew 5). The liberated person may find he is doing the same activities as before—except now with a new motive.

To the person who would walk this liberated life, Christ promises freedom from the heavy burden. However, in its place we will have a light responsibility to bear (*see* Matthew 11:28–30). Therefore, discipline will be a part of our lives, but now it will be done under Christ and for Christ. It will be done out of love and not duty, it will be done because we want to, not because we fear what will happen if we don't (*see* Luke 9:23).

And what are the manifestations of the liberated, Spirit-controlled life? It is of interest to me that the Bible doesn't say the manifestations will be a lot of souls or external works. Rather, the fruits of the Spirit are those of character, i.e., love, joy, peace, patience, kindness, goodness, faithfulness, gentleness, and self-control (*see* Galatians 5:13–23).

DISCUSSION QUESTIONS

°1) Are you a compulsive person, so much so that it is detrimental to you? List the causes.

*2) Are you a legalistic person? List the reasons.

3) Do you agree with the author's reasons for legalism? Which reason(s) is basic to the others and why? Are there any others that should be added to this list?

4) Do you agree that some parts of the Scriptures are relatively more important than other parts? Does this mean that any parts can be neglected? Give some personal examples. What is the risk in making a statement like this?

5) Are there any solutions to legalism which were not listed?

6) Give examples of situations where other people went out of their way to allow you freedom. Do you allow others their freedom?

7) Should a Christian ever "fight" for his freedom? Explain.

8) Is it possible to grieve one Person of the Trinity by overemphasis of another Person in the Trinity? Explain.

9) Explain the paradox of a liberated person having responsibilities.

10) Is it possible there are some forms of legalism in your life you don't recognize? What can be done to make one more sensitive to legalism creeping in?

11) Why might a person be very opinionated? Is there a relationship to compulsiveness and legalism?

12) Why do legalistic leaders fear an emphasis on liberty? Are we better off accepting the problems of legalism than taking the risk of license?

13) Which is preferable to God: a religious legalistic or an indifferent sinner? Why?

13

CRITICAL NEGATIVE ATTITUDES

The world is filled with millions of self-appointed judges who maintain a basically critical and negative attitude about almost everything. They find fault with their neighbors, friends, associates, the church, government leaders, and their pastor. They pass judgment on people, ideas, plans, and doctrine—what is done and what is not done.

Many children see their parents as critical, negative individuals. The criticism may be open and forthright or disguised and subdued, without basis, or supported by a foundation of well-developed logical thought.

Since the negative person is devoting great amounts of energy to being hypercritical, his defenses are well established against any who would try and reckon with him. He dwells on, lives in, and thrives on a critical, negative, often pessimistic frame of mind most of the time. He remembers people's faults instead of their attributes. He points out the problems instead of the potential, sees what is wrong with a plan before he sees its possibilities. He saps a tremendous amount of positive energy from those about him, dampening spirits and crushing possibilities on all sides. It is almost as if he is committed to making his pessimistic outlook come true. This prophet of doom is unhappy and he makes others unhappy. No one pays him for his work but *he* pays dearly for it in the form of disconcerting internal conflict, fatigue, depression, and defeat.

Some negative people consider themselves to be self-appointed policemen and executors of God's judgment. They may be fairly knowledgeable of various subjects, including the Bible, and have a fair amount of insight into others. They might be right in many of their judgments but unloving, thus their entire attitude is essentially wrong. In other words: RIGHT minus LOVE equals WRONG.

The Pharisees repeatedly exemplified this, such as their judgment of the adulterous woman. Christ's comment to them in Matthew 23:23, 24 PHILLIPS is appropriate for today's critics as well:

. . . you utter frauds! For you pay your tithe on mint and aniseed and cummin, and neglect the things which carry far more weight in the Law—justice, mercy and good faith. These are the things you should have observed—without neglecting the others. You call yourselves leaders, and yet you can't see an inch before your noses, for you filter out the mosquito and swallow the camel.

Many critical, negative people legalistically take strong stands on doctrines and codes. They sit back and carefully listen for the least implication involving one of "their" sacred creeds. Now I firmly believe that certain basic doctrines clearly repeated in Scripture should not be compromised. But often it is the less clearly defined areas that upset and consume the energy of the doctrinal critics. These are the doctrines that often split brothers and churches. I often think how easy it would have been for our all-knowing God, who undoubtedly realized this would occur, to have included an extra chapter in the Bible to clarify many of these hazy areas. But maybe He didn't want to. Maybe He wanted to see if we could major on majors and not on minors

128 RUN AND NOT BE WEARY

and prove that love rules in our relationships with our brothers. "I the Lord search the heart, I try the reins, even to give every man according to his ways, and according to the fruit of his doings" (Jeremiah 17:10 KJV).

Why are many of us so prone to judge others and be negative about so many things? Perhaps it is because we are actually guilty (but sometimes totally unaware) of the same thing, or something related to it. Romans 2:1 says: "Therefore you have no excuse, O man, whoever you are, when you judge another; for in passing judgment upon him you condemn yourself, because you, the judge, are doing the very same things." In Christ's example of the judging brother (see Matthew 7), they were both afflicted with the same problem—wood in the eye. The brother with the larger piece not only failed to realize his own need (it was close to his blind spot), but was more ready to see it in his brother and want to help him with his problem.

Another reason we sometimes judge people is to protect other areas in our lives we consciously or unconsciously are trying to keep people from noticing. We may be using the theory that the best defense is an offense. Or perhaps our negativism stems from the fact that we are rigid and legalistic, setting up standards neither we nor anyone else can maintain. People with feelings of inferiority often criticize other people as a way to build themselves up in their own eyes and, they hope, in the eyes of others.

Sometimes critical remarks are a means of releasing energy caused by bitterness, resentment, or hostility within us, possibly about an issue totally unrelated to the issue at hand. A critical attitude can also stem from a jealous, competitive spirit. Out of jealousy Cain killed Abel, Saul tried to kill David and lost God's blessing and His Kingdom, the sorcerer wrongly desired the power of the Holy Spirit, and the Corinthians placed undue emphasis on certain gifts of the Spirit.

Sometimes finding fault with others becomes simply a bad habit because there are so many ears ready to listen. At other times we do it to avoid getting involved in the positive endeavors others are advocating. Taking positive action is work and may leave us open to the criticism of others.

Some people falsely conclude that what is right and appropriate for them must be the same thing God is saying to everyone else. If I interpret what God is saying to me as if God is saying the exact same thing to everyone else, or even *one* other person, I can get both myself and the other person into a lot of trouble.

Let me quickly inject, however, that I am not advocating never looking critically at anything or never saying no. There is an appropriate time, place, and way to evaluate, judge, and take appropriate action. This may involve some criticism. Some people swing to the opposite extreme and are unwilling to fulfill their rightful responsibility along this line. We are admonished in Matthew 7:20 KJV that ". . . by their fruits ye shall know them."

Other verses tell us:

"Don't trust every spirit, dear friends of mine, but test them to discover whether they come from God or not" (1 John 4:1 PHILLIPS).

"By all means use your judgment, and hold on to whatever is really good" (1 Thessalonians 5:21 PHILLIPS).

"A man gifted with the Spirit can judge the worth of everything . . ." (1 Corinthians 2:15 NEB).

The church must be able to appropriately discern between right and wrong (*see* 1 Corinthians 5 and 6) or sin will subtly invade its ranks and the gospel will be hindered. Woe to the man who judges when he should not, and woe to the man who does not judge when he should! This will not always be easy but must be done under God's careful guidance, lovingly and with concern for everyone involved (*see* 2 Corinthians 13:10). Such action must never be vindictive. Rather it must be done after prayerful consideration of the alternatives. Whatever action is taken should be as specific as the surgeon's scalpel which removes only the infected or cancerous area. Then move on to positive pursuits. It didn't take Christ long to throw out the money changers.

How can the negative, critical person become more positive? Remember, all of us tend to slip into this self-defeating state at some time or other.

First, be honest with yourself and openly evaluate your own life for problem areas that need to be resolved (*see* Matthew 7:1–5). Work on your own problems before you try to solve someone else's.

Second, involve yourself in good, constructive pursuits regardless of what the whole world around you is doing. With positive activities to occupy your thoughts you will have much less time to find fault with others. And you will have no reason to defend a lack of purpose in your own life.

Third, sit down with yourself and have a little conference to decide what kind of person you want to be—with God's strength *will* be. Accept the fact that you are hurting others and especially yourself by being negative and critical. Decide how you will actively work on being an optimistic, realistic person. Determine to say nothing that is not pleasing to God and motivated by love. Look for the positive possibilities in each situation and further such wherever you can honestly and sincerely do so.

Some years I have been pretty negative and critical and occasionally I still slip back into the old ways. However, I really want to be a positive person; I am working on building instead of tearing down. And, you know, it's gratifying and often really fun! Realizing what God has done for us, as unworthy as we are, neutralizes any desire to criticize others.

Fourth, if you are in a situation where you sense you are tending to be critical, ask yourself in all honesty, "Why am I reacting this way?" Often you will quickly discover whether the reason is legitimate or not. Sometimes we react because we falsely assume another person's needs, reactions, problems, or interests are exactly like ours.

Several weeks ago I was in a diaconate board meeting. Several members were enthusiastically talking about calling on all the neighbors around our church, showing interest in them, and if possible, sharing the gospel. Though I am basically in favor of this, my first inward reaction was negative. Before speaking (I don't always exercise this much control), I asked myself why I felt so negative toward the idea. The reason, I concluded, was because I thought our next main thrust should be in deepening our relationship with God through Bible study and prayer. Also, I reasoned, if I support this proposal it will imply not only that I am for it, but also that I would actively take part. And I didn't really feel it was what He wanted me to do at this time, with my busy schedule and other things He has laid on my heart.

Then it dawned on me that God motivates people through many different means. Some in our church may respond to calling on neighbors and through this get turned on for Christ. These same people might never get motivated in their Christian life through the best planned fellowship group we could develop. Also, maybe there are many whose basic needs of growth in the Word have been met and their next step of growth should be through outreach. At this juncture I spoke up and heartily encouraged the idea which had been proposed, though I didn't feel I should take an active part in it at this time.

As I am writing this many weeks after the above described meeting, a further question occurs to me. Would my original feelings have been any different if the idea had originated with me?

If, however, in the final analysis you feel that there is a legitimate, rightful, loving basis for your qualms, questions, or criticism, don't repress it. Before speaking, acknowledge the possibility or definite fact in the quietness of your heart. Maybe it should be left there—without taking action or expressing your views. Occasionally it will be necessary to state how you feel, in love, if your comments will be edifying. And sometimes definitive action must be taken under the direction of the Holy Spirit. At times you will try to correct the situation, at other times you will need to simply leave the matter in God's hands. Then quickly return to a positive, optimistic attitude.

Let us therefore stop turning critical eyes on one another. If we must be critical, let us be critical of our own conduct and see that we do nothing to make a brother stumble or fall.

Romans 14:13 PHILLIPS

This love of which I speak is slow to lose patience—it looks for a way of being constructive. It is not possessive; it is neither anxious to impress nor does it cherish inflated ideas of its own importance. Love has good manners and does not pursue selfish advantage. It is not touchy. It does not keep account of evil or gloat over the wickedness of other people. On the contrary, it is glad with all good men when truth prevails. Love knows no limit to its endurance, no end to its trust, no fading of its hope; it can outlast anything. It is, in fact, the one thing that still stands when all else has fallen.

1 Corinthians 13:4–8 PHILLIPS

DISCUSSION QUESTIONS

*1) Do you think you are a critical, negative person? How do others see you?

2) The author makes the statement, "Woe to the man who judges when he should not and woe to the man who does not judge when he should!" Is that contradictory to Matthew 7:1 which tells us, "Judge not that you be not judged"?

3) Do you agree with the equation:

RIGHT   —   LOVE   =   WRONG

Give a personal example of a time you were initially right but due to lack of love became wrong.

4) Why do you think God did not better clarify doctrinal issues that so often divide Christians, thus hindering their effectiveness in accomplishing His work?

5) List the reasons why we are so prone to judge others.

6) What is lost by being critical and negative?

7) Give an example of a time when you reacted negatively to a situation. How might you have handled it more positively?

14

PEOPLE-PLEASING

We all suffer from a tremendous desire and inborn urge to please, to be understood and accepted by others. In its appropriate place this is normal. Certainly as we learn to love people in Christ, an outgrowth of activities will develop that will be pleasing to others.

However, there are some people whose primary purpose in life is to please people. The motivation for their behavior is based on self-love, not primarily on love for others. The external appearance of their activities may be that of self-sacrificing concern for others. However, their real motive is to gain favor, praise, understanding, acceptance, approval, and love for themselves. They are highly self-centered. "People-pleasers" feel they must have the approval and praise of others, regardless of the cost.

Many of our social obligations fall under the category of people-pleasing. We attend certain meetings and functions, not because we really want to or because our presence will be of help to anyone. We go because we have been asked, and we are afraid we will offend someone if we turn him down.

Certainly we should not be rude to people. As Christians we

must have a high degree of sensitivity to the needs of those around us. However, some people are overly sensitive to the needs and opinions of others to the point of being pathological. They spend a lot of time thinking, "What does so-and-so think of me? What does he expect of me? How can I please him?" These thoughts may be so automatic, even unconscious, the person doesn't even realize he is a people-pleaser.

People-pleasing is a wearisome task. It leads to tremendous internal conflict with the inevitable result of fatigue. The uncertainty of wondering what people really think of us produces anxiety and even depression if we think we have lost another person's esteem.

The people-pleaser does not know his own mind because he is always trying to figure out what other people want him to do or be. This forces him to continually wear a mask. Ironic as it may seem, he usually keeps other people at arm's distance. He wants a lot of admirers—at a distance—because he fears that closeness will expose him. This robs him of close friendships and close relationships with his own family because the closer people get the more likely they are to see behind his mask of self-centeredness and self-love. Often legitimate family needs and even his own needs will go ignored as he frantically tries to impress his more distant audience. If he continues in his role of trying to please people, he will never know God's will and potential for him. Jesus said, "How on earth can you believe [have faith] while you are for ever looking for one another's approval and not for the glory [honor] that comes from the one God?" (John 5:44 PHILLIPS).

Because the people-pleaser has never been involved in wholesome, loving, giving relationships he may in the end lose everything—God, family, and all his coveted admirers. Balaam is a good example of this. He was a prophet who communicated with God and was advised by God not to return with King Balak's honored men. But the people pressed him and with the allurement of personal gain he finally yielded. The result was a trouble-filled trip with both God and King Balak angry at him. His acts cost him his life (*see* Numbers 22–24, 31). If the people-pleaser had gone God's way, seeking Him above all else, he could have learned true love and acceptance—first from God and then from others and even from himself. In the end he would have pleased God and may, in fact, have pleased many people, although the latter should be an incidental result rather than a primary motivating factor.

Brother Lawrence, in *The Practice of the Presence of God,* puts us on the right track in dealing with this problem. He exhorts, "I began to live as if there was none but He [God] and I in the world."

At first glance this statement may seem like he was totally inconsiderate of the needs of those around him. However, nothing could be further from the truth. Brother Lawrence simply knew how to put first things first. We must be willing to sacrifice every good thought people have about us in order to seek God's favor. This will mean saying no to certain requests and at times being misunderstood. God will occasionally test us to see just who has first place in our hearts.

Each of us must be willing to die to the people around us and follow God alone—the *living* God. If we are unwilling to do this we will suffer great loss. Saul lost his entire kingdom because of people-pleasing (*see* 1 Samuel 15:17). A people-pleaser is actually licked before he gets started. He can never please one person all of the time or all of the people part of the time. And certainly he never pleases God or himself. So he must choose. Will he serve God—or man?

People-pleasing can be a particular problem for the Christian, I think, because we may feel we are hurting others and not showing love if we don't try to please them. Some might retort, "Isn't pleasing others a way of showing love?" At times it is, but only if our primary motivation is to please God. As we learn to live by principles of love and concern under the direction of the Holy Spirit our thoughts will change from, "What will that person think of me?" to, "How can God best use me to help that person in love?" We will evaluate our basic responsibilities and priorities in the light of God's will. Ultimately we may have to choose at times between saying no and being misunderstood or saying yes and being disobedient to Christ.

Is anyone free from the tendency to be people-pleasers? At times all of us face this temptation. The more we commit the problem to God, however, the sooner we will be able to say with Jesus: ". . . I always do what is pleasing to him [God]" (John 8:29), and with Paul: "So we speak, not to please men, but to please God who tests our hearts" (1 Thessalonians 2:4). (*See also* Galatians 1:10; Ephesians 6:5, 6; Matthew 6:1; Luke 9:23–25.) And then we will be able to properly carry out Romans 15:2 which says: "Let each of us please his neighbor for his good to edify him." As God refines our hearts He will teach us His love and concern for His world. In the process we will become integrated, whole people with more energy, whose primary motivation is to please God.

DISCUSSION QUESTIONS

*1) Are you more concerned with (a) what people think of you, or (b) what God thinks? Be honest with yourself.

*2) Are you overly sensitive? List why.

3) Are there times when we should be sensitive to what others think of us? Give an example.

4) Where is the line between properly pleasing others and people-pleasing?

5) Why will a people-pleaser eventually not know his own mind?

6) What happens within the family relationships if one or both parents are people-pleasers?

7) If a person stops being a people-pleaser will he be inconsiderate and rude towards others?

8) What new problems will the people-pleaser face when he breaks the old thought patterns?

15

THE SECULAR-SPIRITUAL CONFLICT

Another frequent dilemma for the person desiring to please Christ is that so much of his activities, he thinks, are secular and not spiritual. The housewife washing dishes and changing diapers, the businessman selling insurance, and the mechanic repairing automobiles sometimes do not see how their jobs are furthering the Kingdom of God. Tasks involved in supplying our material needs are considered to be of the world and seemingly insignificant. In fact, some Christians often feel that such tasks are intruders, forcing them to cut out truly spiritual activities. This attitude often leads to doing these tasks grudgingly or at least not "heartily as unto the Lord" as we are commanded in Colossians 3:23. The individual may wonder if he is in God's will and perhaps become resentful. In his mind he is a second-class Christian because he is not able to spend more time in important "spiritual" activities.

How does the secular-spiritual conflict cause fatigue? In my opinion it creates unresolved internal conflict in at least five ways which often lead to fatigue. First of all it can cause false guilt and confusion by implying that we are second-rate, not completely yielded Christians if we are not "full time." Second, if we aren't careful we can look at our secular job as unimportant or even a necessary evil. The poor attitude that tends to follow this type of thinking drains us of vital energy (*see* chapter 21). Third, if we feel that we have to do secular work to meet our financial responsibilities, it is easy for bitterness and resentment to creep in with the host of problems they create (*see* chapter 8). Fourth, we may try and crowd in as many spiritually important activities as possible in every free moment when we are not engaged in secular work. This leads to a weary, frantic pace. Fifth, it may lead to our giving up. After all, what's the use if most of our productive hours are engaged in this world's activities? This attitude is sin and leads to true guilt with all its consequences.

Many people are driven into so-called full-time Christian work because they are unable to resolve this dilemma. However, before long they find that the same "unspiritual" type of work comes back to haunt them. A missionary arrives on the mission field, eager to preach and teach. To his surprise he finds he must spend hours and hours building houses, fixing plumbing, and doing other mundane tasks he may have thought were unspiritual. Hopefully, before long he discovers that "full-time" work has little bearing on the basic issue of the secular-spiritual conflict.

The way the word *full-time* is used in Christian circles is not only a misnomer, it actually accentuates the secular-spiritual conflict for both the full-timer and the layman. It tends to denote certain people and specific activities as being the spiritual ones that count. Both groups tend to see the layman's role as less than spiritual, possibly implying his apparent unwillingness to sell out for Christ. This kind of attitude hinders fellowship and may even foster a type of snobbishness, one person or group looking down upon another. If God should suddenly call a full-timer to temporarily "make tents" (do secular work for a while to meet his material needs) the issue is further confused.

Before we go any further, let's define our terms. *Secular* means literally to belong to an age or generation. It means belonging to this temporal world. It is worldly and deprived of religious character. It has to do with the physical. When used by religious people it often also implies that which is less-important and even sensual. "Spiritual," on the other hand, refers to the spirit or soul as distinguished from the body. It may refer to intellect, refinement of thought, as well as that which is sacred. The religious person often uses it to imply all the important things in life. It stands for eternal and lasting quality.

Many individuals equate "sold out to God" with "full time." After all, the disciples left their worldly occupations to follow Christ. Can we expect to do any less? Weren't the great men in the Scriptures all full time? The answer is NO. Many great men and women in the Scriptures had full-time secular jobs. They did not get financial pay for administering God's work. Abraham was a traveler, businessman, and rancher, but was considered a "friend of God" and is listed with many other laymen in the hall of faith of Hebrews 11. Joseph was a slave, servant, prisoner, and finally minister of agriculture for all of Egypt and these became the means of fulfilling God's plan. David was a shepherd, soldier, and successful leader of a nation and not a full-time priest with the rights of priesthood. But no full-timer was called a "man after mine own heart" by God as David was. Esther was the First Lady of Persia but had time and courage to risk her life to be God's instrument in saving a nation. And the anonymous homemaker in Proverbs 31 was praised for her ability and long, hard hours of sewing, weaving, obtaining groceries, cooking, and for using wisdom in economic matters of the household. She loved God, had an excellent relationship with her husband and children, was kind, responded to the needs of the poor, and had a good attitude toward her domestic responsibilities. The Scriptures comment: "Many women have done excellently, but you surpass them all." Did she miss her "calling"? I think not.

And there are New Testament examples of lay people fully responding to God's call. Lydia, a saleslady who apparently was single, was open to God and appears to have been instrumental in the establishment of the church at Philippi (*see* Acts 16). Cornelius found that being a full-time military officer in no way hindered his receptivity to God. And there are many others such as Lazarus, who was deeply loved by Christ yet wasn't called to leave his home and follow Him, and Stephen, the waiter, whose life was so filled with God and His Word that he was the first martyr for his faith (*see* Acts 6, 7).

As one reads through the Scriptures it doesn't seem to make much difference whether the individual was in full-time service to God or not. What mattered was that God was the most important thing in his life. I might hasten to add that there were undoubtedly thousands of priests and other full-timers living in the days and area of the recorded events of the Scriptures. Most of these are never mentioned. Many full-timers, however, are noted in the Scriptures for their indifference or for actually hindering the work of God. So, full-time work is absolutely no guarantee of a close relationship with God or His blessing. For the most part it is not the number of hours one spends in serving or working for God that count, it is his degree of devotion to God. Both the full-timer and the layman are equally responsible for deep growth in their spiritual lives, knowing and applying His Word, and continued obedience in all that He directs (*see* Acts 6, 7).

Brother Lawrence went to a monastery in the seventeenth century to find God. And what spiritual task was he given? For fifteen years he cooked meals and washed dishes, a task for which he had a natural aversion. But he "accustomed himself to do everything there for the love of God and with prayer, upon all occasions, for His grace to do His work well, he found everything easy. . . . We find him worshipping more in his kitchen than in his cathedral; he could pray with another, 'Lord of all pots and pans and things, make me a saint by getting meals and washing up the plates.'" And he could say, "The time of business does not with me differ from the time of prayer." He sought God, "not even his gifts."

How many Brother Lawrences are there today, whether in or out of full-time work, who have not seen "their kitchen" as a spiritual task, and thus have not done it unto the Lord? They must be of all men most miserable. I often wonder if it isn't our pride that makes us unwilling to see God's hand in the seemingly small task, all the while holding out for some great spiritual work.

To resolve the spiritual-secular conflict we must see every activity we undertake as *God's* activity. Any work is spiritual when done as unto Him. The only exception is work where our willful sin is involved. This, of course, can take any form—an activity that is out of His will or a job that usurps too much importance or time. If sin is present we must confess it, take appropriate action, and then go on in our walk with Him. "To the pure all things are pure" (Titus 1:15). This elevates the most mundane activity.

But more important than seeing the tasks we do as His, is maintaining the continuing fellowship with Christ throughout the day whenever our thoughts can be freed from the task at hand. Thus, we are periodically aligning ourselves to God in a conscious way. A. W. Tozer says in *The Pursuit of God,* "It is not what a man does that determines whether his work is sacred or secular, it is why he does it." This makes all of life His—our time, money, possessions, and our own personal sense of worth. It is no longer a certain amount of time or money given to His work; it is ALL His and we are His stewards. Then we can see every task as spiritual—opportunities to share the gospel with others, responsibilities at home and on the job, and even an appropriate amount of fun and pleasure. In Christ's day even the slaves were guaranteed this fact and were told to obey their earthly master from the heart. Though they were heartily serving man, they were motivated by love for Christ and their reward would be for serving the Lord (*see* Colossians 3:22–24). In 1 Corinthians 7:20–24 they were told to be content right where they were, but if opportunity for advancement came they should avail themselves of it.

All then is spiritual except sin if truly done unto God.

DISCUSSION QUESTIONS

1) Is anything (apart from one's own sin) in the Christian's life not spiritual?

2) What aspects or areas of your life do you consider to be more spiritual than others? How does this type of thinking drain one of energy?

3) Why is the term "full-time Christian work" a misnomer?

4) In which role do you think it is easier for a person to be a truly yielded Christian: missionary, minister, housewife, laborer, business or professional man?

5) Suppose a man undertakes a job under God's direction—say starting his own business. Now, however, he is working fifty or more hours a week and has little time for God or family. How can he resolve his secular-spiritual conflict?

6) How do the Scripture teachings about gifts (see 1 Corinthians 12–14) apply to the secular-spiritual conflict?

16

THE URGE TO MAKE AND BECOME FOLLOWERS

Once upon a time there was a large prosperous group of people whom God directed and blessed. But they weren't satisfied. They wanted a leader, organization, and stature. This desire persisted despite warnings from one lone man who happened to know God's will in the matter. Finally God gave in. Their leader was a capable and "handsome young man" and God blessed this second-best arrangement as long as both leader and followers obeyed Him. Despite God's favor and the people's high respect, the leader felt inadequate. He, in fact, built a "monument for himself." He was also a people-pleaser because he feared his followers. Possibly because of his insecurities he overcompensated by doing an extra, worthy, religious service which not only wasn't required, but in fact was contrary to God's will. This greatly displeased God and proved to be the beginning of the end for the leader. In the course of events the leader made a rule which, incidentally, was totally unnecessary. But this rule robbed the followers of vitally necessary energy, leaving them exhausted. In addition it directly caused the followers to sin against God and led to a dispute within the leader's family.

All of these factors not only strained the leader's relationship with God but produced tremendous internal turmoil, jealousy, confusion, and weariness. It ultimately cost him his life. The followers also had their share of difficulties during the rule of the leader. (Read carefully chapters 8 through 31 of 1 Samuel for further details.)

The urge to make and become followers also occurs in the New Testament. Mark 9:38–42 says, "John said to him, 'Teacher, we saw a man casting out demons in your name, and we forbade him, because he was not following us.' But Jesus said, 'Do not forbid him. . . .'" And in 1 Corinthians 3:3–9 Paul says, "For while there is jealousy and strife among you, are you not of the flesh, and behaving like ordinary men? For when one says, 'I belong to Paul,' and another, 'I belong to Apollos,' are you not merely men?"

In all of life's arenas, the urge to make and become followers is apparent. Politically, there is the cause or the candidate to support. One church competes with another, or one denomination with another which, unfortunately, may even cause splits within a church, creating a tremendous drain of talent, energy, and resources. Even within families there is the urge to have Junior follow Dad's profession and to cut his hair the same length. To make or become followers is an intrinsic urge within all of us to a greater or lesser degree. In a few people this is a great problem —it may be their major problem. To most of the rest of us it may be only a minor and infrequent, but sometimes subtle and unrecognized problem.

How does the urge to make or become followers produce fatigue? To the would-be leader (who may be a person trying to get his neighbor to follow him or the established head of a large movement) seeking a following, he may manipulate, people-please, hide his true self behind a mask, resort to legalism, or devise some great plan or organization to achieve his desired end. He may ultimately sin rather than risk losing his following. All of these internal-conflict producers are discussed in accompanying chapters.

The follower of a man, plan, or organization may also develop tremendous fatigue. He is more prone to people-please his leader, lose sight of Christ, and become entangled in mechanics or legalism. The mask serves as a means of shielding his weaknesses from his exalted leader. The leader may become an unconscious idol negating the leading of the Holy Spirit in his life. The follower is often pushed into a constricting mold for which he was never intended. All of which will produce internal conflict with its many possible results, including fatigue.

Does this mean that the urge to make or become followers is always wrong? By no means! Christ called unto Himself His disciples and they followed Him and learned to grow. Paul had his followers and exhorted others to: "Be ye followers of me, even as I also am of Christ" (1 Corinthians 11:1 KJV). Several times in my life key individuals had a tremendous positive effect on me and for a while I was a follower of them. It is like a parent teaching his children. But as time passes, a good parent will teach the child to mature and to be less dependent upon humans. So it is with us. We must learn to grow up. Though we may follow men for a period of time, we ultimately must raise our sight to Christ.

What are some of the mechanisms used in Christendom to make followers? First, there is the doctrinal emphasis—some slight variation of emphasis on a doctrine. People are then judged as either in or out of this doctrinal group. It may not be a wrong doctrine. It can even be a correct doctrine rightly applied, but if overemphasized it can distort its relative importance with respect to the whole counsel and teachings of God. This is especially true if love is lacking. An equation might be:

TRUTH + OVEREMPHASIS = WRONG

The Pharisees and scribes were guilty of this. They missed the entire revelation of God, though holding avidly to the Scriptures. Denominations may become guilty of this. Most of the epistles were written to resolve some problem along this line (*see* chapter 12).

The second mechanism used to make followers is that of an experience. It may be a certain emotional feeling with salvation or a predefined means to prove God vindicates one's faith. It may be to expect a miraculous healing. Some teach certain "gifts" are necessary to prove that one has been filled with the Holy Spirit. The church in Corinth was guilty of this more than other churches and, incidentally, was the most immature of the churches. This does not mean that an experience is not a wonderful event, but it must never become a sought-after idol or a source of division between brethren. The sorcerer in Acts 8:9–25 was strongly rebuked for wanting self-centered spiritual power.

The third mechanism used to make followers is a plan or strategy. A plan can be a tremendous thing—how to grow in the Word, how to evangelize, a unique Bible study and sharing group, a church, a mission. These plans may lead to forming organizations. However, any of these can degenerate into something which actually distracts from God (*see* chapters 12, 17, and 18).

The question you may be asking is, why do some people have the urge to make followers? Obviously, it can have its proper place. The essence of the great commission is to make disciples. However, its aim is to make disciples of Christ and His will—not disciples of ourselves or our persuasions. It must be for the good of the follower and to glorify Jesus Christ. If it ever ceases to have the best interests of the follower at heart, then it must be questioned. Unfortunately, the urge to make followers may be motivated out of a need to verify the leader's belief, to avoid the threat of failure, or to combat insecurities within the leader. Sometimes it is for financial reasons or for power, authority, and ego-gratification. Remember, the last idol many of us must defeat is the monument to self.

Why do people want to become followers? This, too, can be quite proper. Someone who is young may need to identify with another person in order to grow in Christ. Timothy followed Paul, Elisha followed Elijah. There are also legitimate times when a group of people can organize and do a better job collectively then individually (see chapters 17 and 18).

On the other hand, following a person or group can occur without any awareness of what is happening to the naïve follower. It is easier to follow a person or promote a plan, a cause, or an emphasis than to be Christ's person being led by the Holy Spirit. The follower who is associated with some great person, plan, or movement gains stature and worth. This may help alleviate his insecurities. However, he may fail to see that being a follower of men can interfere with his relationship to Christ.

Followers are particularly vulnerable to how they perceive others—whether leaders, organizations, church, or spouse. How we all perceive others changes. The other person may not change —but how we perceive him changes. This has a tremendous effect on him and on us. The person who is prone to be a follower is also prone to wide swings in how he sees others. Understanding this about himself can help him deal with it and the problems it creates.

Typically there are three ways we may perceive a person, leader, group, organization, church, or even our own spouse. I call these the THREE PHASES OF PERCEPTION. First, is phase one, which I call the ADORATION PHASE. This is a phase where the adored person (or group) is the greatest thing in the world to the follower. He is held in high devotion, almost to the point of worship. Seemingly, he can do no wrong. The follower often cannot understand why others do not see him the same way he does. During this courting or honeymoon phase, the person or organization wields a tremendous amount of control over his followers, sometimes to the point of weariness. The follower also can easily slip into the people-pleasing problems enumerated previously. God can be demoted to second place, sometimes without the leader or the follower realizing what is happening. Usually the adoration phase doesn't last. Imperfect humans will ultimately goof. God usually will not permit an organization or a person to stay in the highest esteem very long without His intervening. The follower will move from this phase into phase two, which I call the DISILLUSIONED PHASE.

Now only the faults and the problems of the leader or group are seen by the follower, often with resentment, hostility, and bitterness. Whether he holds this in or verbalizes it, the follower hurts himself and many others, causing tremendous internal conflicts and often fatigue. The person who rose high on the crest of the adoration phase often finds himself deep in the gully of the disillusioned phase. If the follower lost sight of God in phase one, he certainly will lose sight of Him in phase two. Many individuals, unfortunately, stay in this phase the rest of their lives. Some find a new leader or cause to start the adoration phase over again, often never learning to see things realistically. Others may proceed directly to phase three. Whether the person goes through phase one and two is not as important as that he move on to phase three, which I call the REALISTIC PHASE.

In this phase the follower accepts leaders, organizations, and the church as they are, sees their stronger and weaker features without distorting them. Unfortunately, many people never reach this phase. God never used a perfect man or organization to perform His will, apart from Christ. You see, He has only imperfect people like you and me available to Him. He could have chosen to use His angels but He did not. His plan included imperfect vessels so that He might be magnified.

Think for a moment of the faults of David and his sin of adultery, the disciples in their self-seeking, Peter in his denial of Christ, Paul, or, for that matter, the entire early church. They all had their faults, but think also of their good points and remember that God used them all. Remember, also, that we see other people, organizations, and the church through our own eyes. They have blind spots, near and far vision, astigmatism, and all the other distortions which we superimpose. God alone really knows another person. Therefore, we should learn to be as realistic as possible about others. This will also help us be realistic about ourselves.

What is the solution to the general problem of the urge to make or become followers? As mentioned several times, the urge to make or become followers can have its appropriate place and should not be condemned by any means. Leaders are especially responsible to constantly point to Christ and encourage others as they mature to cut the apron strings and depend more upon Christ and less upon them. They must realize that relationships that are too dependent (although it may be ego-gratifying) eventually will hurt both leader and follower and the cause of Christ. Leaders must be aware that God's mold for everyone is slightly different and they should not be discouraged if their followers see things slightly differently. The leader must always have the follower's individual best interest at heart.

The follower should likewise see that imitating a leader can be helpful for a while and a means of growth; but his prime relationship must be more and more with the person of Jesus Christ. This does not mean that one cannot work with others and be *conditionally* subject to them. Remember that Christ wants to be the prime leader in your life—so be leery of anyone or anything that interferes with that relationship. Are you willing above all else to be a follower of Christ?

DISCUSSION QUESTIONS

°1) Have you ever felt that Christian friends, a fellowship group, the church, or an organization has tried to make you a follower of them more than of Christ? Give an example.

2) Do you agree with the author's reasons why leaders have the urge to make followers? List the reasons and add others that he might have missed.

3) Is the author too hard on leaders?

4) Are there any experiences in the Christian life intended for everyone? List.

5) Did the author take unjustified liberties in illustrating King Saul's life in the first portion of this chapter?

6) Have you ever been a follower when you shouldn't have been? Describe.

*7) Do you think ulterior motives creeping up in Christian leaders are (a) rare; (b) occasional; (c) common.

8) Have you gone through the Adoration, Disillusioned and Realistic phases? Give a personal example of each. Do you think we can mature to the point of not having to go through the first two phases in future relationships? Has your marriage gone through these phases?

17

THE PLAN

Martha Martyr is a faithful member of The Fellowship of the Faithful Few. You can always count on her, she sings in the choir, is deaconness, and can always be relied on to make calls. She is active in the women's auxiliary, and this month their special project is to collect and pack barrels of slightly used tea bags and out-of-style clothing to send to the missionaries in Africa. She also teaches a Sunday-school class of seven-year-old boys— she really prefers twelve-year-old girls but there is no one else willing to try and handle the rowdy seven-year-old boys. If there is a function at church, you can count on her being there, and many times she is helping the pastor or someone else during the day.

Deacon Alwaysright is also a member of The Fellowship of the Faithful Few. In fact, he is virtually singularly responsible for its organization. He had a little problem about a doctrinal issue in the church down the street which caused him to realize that none of the ten churches in the town had their doctrinal issues straight. Some were off in teachings regarding the Holy Spirit, others had their timing on the millennium fouled up, and

151

still others were all wet on baptism. Deacon Alwaysright contacted the denominational headquarters and they fully agreed that though this was considered an overchurched town, certainly the truth should be taught someplace in this community.

The first five years the church grew and seemed to prosper. However, the last five years has been marked by a steady decline. Last Tuesday night a special business meeting was called to reevaluate the situation and to develop a "five-year plan." At one point it was kind of tense! Mr. Naïve Young Christian—the only convert in three years—and he came through a friend—asked if possibly something had gone wrong with God's plan for the fellowship. It was a good thing that Bishop Stock Answer had come from headquarters, because after a few moments of deadening silence, he stood up and, in his usual authoritarian manner, asked a series of interesting and provocative questions.

First of all, he asked, "Did the Lord call you to start The Fellowship of the Faithful Few?"

Deacon Alwaysright quickly stood and vouched for that. It took him fifteen minutes to reiterate God's call for a doctrinally correct church in this sinful community and the glorious days of God's outpouring.

"Why, remember," he said, "the one night alone when the visiting evangelist came and twenty went forward?" By the time Deacon Alwaysright finished, the tenseness which had settled over the congregation had passed.

Then Bishop Stock Answer asked his second question: "Does God ever change His mind?"

Fortunately, Mary Pious came through for a change. Usually she won't help in any of the work that needs to be done, but she reaffirmed for them all, that God never changes His mind for, "We have a changeless God." She even quoted the reference.

Then the Bishop went on to say: "Are you willing to be faithful to the task that God has called you to?" He gave a sermonette about the little boy with his insignificant two loaves and five fish and that anything given to the Master will be used and multiplied. He also refreshed their memories about the parable of the talents. Only the person who has been faithful over a few things will be made ruler over many things. He reminded them that God's Word goes from their pulpit each week and it would never return void. He then had them all stand to reaffirm their willingness to continue the important work of The Fellowship of the Faithful Few. Everyone quickly stood, except there seemed to be a certain hesitancy and confusion written all over the face of Mr. Naïve Young Christian. But shortly he joined the rest of the congregation.

Well, soon the business meeting moved on and it was voted to have a Friday-night fellowship dinner and Bible study. They figured that serving food would help get people out for the Bible study. Deacon Alwaysright agreed to teach Revelation again—he had some new insights on it since last year when he taught it for Wednesday-night Bible study and the year before when he taught it for the adult Sunday-school class. However, desperately needed was someone to be in charge of serving the dinner. Finally, Martha Martyr willingly agreed. She had initially hoped that the Bishop's fine talk would motivate Mary Pious and Jane Indifferent to volunteer, but when they didn't she did, because "there was no one else" to do this vitally important task. In fact, Martha had hoped that Mary and Jane would at least feel guilty enough to assist her. After all, didn't they know that Martha never has time with her family as it is and is exhausted already?

Down the street from The Fellowship of the Faithful Few is "The Congregation of the Successful." They don't have any of the problems of the congregation of the faithful few. Their numbers increase each year. Their budget is gigantic. Their program won't stop, and to sit in one of their services is better entertainment than the local theater and it doesn't cost as much.

Five years ago it started with Reverend P. R. Promoter. He came to town with a great plan in mind, and did it ever work! They have people from almost every other church in town. He would have been good at most any job whether salesman or corporation president. He is very capable. I understand that his board agrees with virtually everything he wants. If they don't, they are soon moved to another position.

These fictitious stories illustrate how plans *may* go wrong. The Fellowship of the Faithful Few illustrates what I call "the syndrome of the faithful few." This is where faithfulness is elevated to an almost sacred quality. Of course, there are many verses throughout the Bible which exemplify faithfulness. We as Christians should be reliable, trustworthy, and faithful to commitments. There may be times when we have to be faithful through many lean months or years in obedience to His will. However, our faithfulness must always be to Christ. Faithfulness to a person, plan, organization, or church must never be our final goal.

Some people are faithful for the sake of being faithful which is another form of legalism. Very often people are faithful because their ego is at stake. Sometimes I have wished the faithful few were not so faithful. They are often very reliable and trustworthy, but fail to see that pruning is a necessary and absolute part in the Christian life and that God's will is dynamic. Those who become involved in the Syndrome of the Faithful Few are often well-meaning, hard-working, but very weary, legalistic individuals. They have little joy. They sap tremendous amounts of energy from themselves and others. They create frustrating problems and confusion of loyalties.

The Congregation of the Successful, on the other hand, illustrates the erroneous idea (in my opinion) that "success means God's approval." Many Christians seem to think that if something is successful, whether it is a Bible study, youth program, witnessing approach, musical group, or church as a whole, it must be of God. Success vindicates action only if the success is what God wants and the way He wants it done. Not only must the end be what God wants, but the means to the end.

An interesting but tragic example of this is when God provided water for the children of Israel from the rock. In Numbers 20:8–12, Moses was told to speak to the rock. But instead he struck the rock. Nothing happened the first time so he struck it again, using more energy, and interestingly it says ". . . water came forth abundantly." The end was right but the means was wrong. God performed a miracle and caused abundant success. But the same stroke that caused success was a stroke of disobedience which ultimately prevented Moses from entering the Promised Land. God had told him to take his rod with him, but specifically to speak to the rock on this second occasion. The rod was given to Moses to demonstrate God's mighty power. This was, in a sense, Moses' symbolic strongpoint. But it became the point of Moses' disobedience and God's great displeasure.

This may seem like a small point until we realize that speaking and striking the rock were not the issue, but rather carefully listening to God's voice and following Him instead of being stuck on a plan. Moses was disobedient because he was, in fact, adhering to a previous plan of God's. The first time the Israelites needed water God's chosen plan was that Moses was to strike the rock which produced the desired results. The second time the need was the same, the situation the same, the tools available were the same—but God changed the plan slightly. Unfortunately, Moses wasn't carefully listening. To obey God is more important than the noblest activity, work, or final results that one could achieve (see 1 Samuel 15:17-24). To the reader who is still not convinced that success does not necessarily mean God's blessing, I suggest you read Matthew 6:21-23.

My aim is not to decry either the faithful or the successful, but to point out that in either case the individual may become more enamored with plans than with the Planner. When this happens people become weary and sometimes get crushed in the machinery of the program.

However, plans have a place. Reading the Scriptures carefully, one finds that God has a master plan, which includes the Jewish nation, Christ, the Apostles, and us today. God has specific plans for different ages and people.

Plans are like tools. They can be indispensable or destructive. For example, it is almost impossible for even the best carpenter to build a house of wood and nails without a hammer. But, when used indiscriminately, that same hammer can give a deathblow.

So it is with plans. If they become an end in themselves, if they are rigidly held to, they can put people into molds. They can mow over people and lead to a tremendous amount of fatigue, discouragement, depression, and confusion.

What are some of the problems with plans? Obviously, no plan or the wrong plan will result in shipwreck. But what about the right plan? What can go wrong with this plan? First of all, we can become stuck on a plan and think there is only one way to do God's work. Moses was stuck on a plan as to how God would supply water. In *Evangelism*, G. Campbell Morgan wrote, "If a man is praying for an old-fashioned revival, in all probability when God's visitation comes, he will not be conscious of it." He goes on to say that revivals are different, they start in different ways and have different characteristics of the same basic message. However, if a person has a stereotyped idea of how God would send a revival, he will probably miss the one God sends.

Secondly, we can goof up the right plan by allowing our ego to get attached to the plan. Jonah is a good example. God had a plan for his life that included warning the people of Nineveh of God's impending judgment. Jonah resisted God's plan and it caused him all sorts of difficulty and fatigue. Finally, in the pit of despair, he sought God's help—and gave thanks—and then God delivered him. God gave Jonah a second chance to follow His will, and this time he was obedient; warning the sinful Ninevites. To Jonah's surprise, this wicked city responded, resulting in God changing His plan for the city. But Jonah was rigid. He was unwilling to accept God's change. His ego and possible "what will they think of me" got involved. These became more important to him than all the lives in Nineveh and God's will. Jonah got angry, depressed, and faint because of this internal conflict. God had changed the plan, and Jonah couldn't—no, *wouldn't*—adjust.

The children of Israel wandering in the wilderness are another example of getting attached to a plan. They started out in obedience and ended up yielding to the weakness of the flesh. Had you asked them if they were God's people and in His will they would probably have said yes. They could proudly point to all the mighty works God had done for them, that He was still leading them with the cloud by day and the pillar of fire by night, and sustaining them by the miracle of manna from heaven. Here again, apparent blessing does not tell the whole story, because their disobedience forced God to lead them in circles while waiting for a new generation.

What begins with God's blessing may even become an instrument of evil. The bronze serpent (see Numbers 21:8, 9) was God's chosen means of deliverance. Later, the Israelites failed to see that it was only an instrument. It became an idol and King Hezekiah (see 2 Kings 18:4) had to destroy it.

Paul dealt with the early church over this same issue. "Having begun with the Spirit," he said, "are you now ending with the flesh?" (Galatians 3:3).

Impatience is another way our carnal lives can overthrow a spiritual plan. Abraham was promised a son, an heir, but he became impatient and tried in his own way to help God's plan along. He got a son all right—Ishmael—and also a lot of problems.

We are probably all guilty at times of resorting to the flesh in trying to carry out God's plan. I remember when my days in the navy were drawing to a close, I spent scores of hours evaluating, praying, and seeking God's will for the future. To the best of my knowledge, I was willing to go into the ministry, mission field, or any "secular" area where I could live for Him.

Eventually, God led me into medicine. This pleased me but left me apprehensive because competition was stiff. I had done well in undergraduate studies, had ended with a scholarship and assurances from those who knew me and the medical curriculum that I would do well, which ultimately proved to be true. However, I did not know the future, and though led by God into medicine, I took the burden on myself; my ego got involved with the horrible fear of flunking out. Thus, I had many weary, dry months, leaving me with the scar of an ulcer. I started out fine but was trying to complete it in my own strength. I was unwilling to consider the possibility that God might change His plan midstream. Fortunately, we can realign our lives with His will at any time, which I have subsequently done; but our disobedience will often leave its scars.

What is the solution to plans and the problems they may create? First, of course, we must realize that plans are tremendous tools and, in their place, are a vital part of the Christian life. However, we must start with Christ, continue with Christ, and end with Christ. Christ must always be more important than all of our plans or strategy.

Second, obedience to Christ and all that that involves, as we've discussed throughout this book, is absolutely necessary. The chapter on legalism is especially applicable.

Third is the full appreciation that God's will and plan for our lives is dynamic. Not static. I want to dwell on this in some detail because it is so important in resolving the problems that inherently can creep into the best-laid plans and in living a free, energetic, Holy-Spirit-led life. You see, I believe God's will or plan for our lives—or His will about any plan—may *seem to change*.

It may seem to change if we were actually wrong in what we thought His will was for us in the first place. As soon as we realize that, we should quickly admit it while He is giving us a second chance to realign our will with His.

Or it may seem to change at times when He is testing us. He may have to occasionally test us to see if our desire to please Him is greater than the plan. Abraham had to be totally willing to give up his greatest possession—Isaac—who embodied both God's and Abraham's hope for the future. Only when Abraham proved willing was it revealed that God had no intention of actually taking Isaac.

Another way that God's will and plan for our lives may seem to change is when we read into His plan far more than He intended. We may assume things He never told us. To illustrate the point, I live in a suburb of Los Angeles and a mile north of us is the San Diego Freeway. God may some day direct me to get on the San Diego Freeway and head south. Now, it would be easy for me to assume that He wants me to go to San Diego, but He did not tell me that. Ten miles down the road, He may, in "a still small voice," tell me to turn off the freeway in Long Beach. If I have my eyes focused on San Diego and am merrily driving along, I may be many miles beyond the turnoff before I sense an uneasiness and realize I might be out of His will. I can remain confused if I fail to see that God only told me to get on the freeway and did not tell me what the end point was.

My brother, Paul, also illustrates this point. He felt "called" to go to the Congo, signed up for a four-year term, and implied a longer commitment. But God only allowed him to be there eighteen months before He took him home. God often unfolds His will to us only a step at a time (*see* Genesis 12:1).

God's will is dynamic to the point that *it may actually at times change.* In my opinion and on carefully reading the Scriptures, if we deny God this right we not only limit God and misunderstand His character, but also create confusion and possible sin for ourselves. Admittedly it may not occur very often. It probably only occurs in response to a change man has made. This is a necessary result of His allowing us humans to act as free agents having our own wills and the option of choice within certain bounds. The point, however, is that His will is dynamic and it may occasionally change. We put God in a restricting mold if we deny Him this right.

You may reply that this is heresy; we have a changeless God who knows the end from the beginning (*see* Malachi 3:6). He has no reason to change. We are reminded in Hebrews 6:17 that even His purposes are unchangeable. His Word tells us, "For truly, I say to you, till heaven and earth pass away, not an iota, not a dot, will pass from the law until all is accomplished" (Matthew 5:18).

So God cannot change; and I would agree there are many things which are unchangeable. Christ, Himself, despite His prayer and agony, could not change the mind of God in the Garden of Gethsemane to alter God's plan of salvation and redemption for mankind. God's character, the fact of sin, the penalty which must be paid for sin, His basic timetable—these are only a few of the things which will never change. God has established these and certain other statutes. To change them He would have to change His character and go back on His already spoken Word—something He will never do. There will always be certain unchangeable precepts. But to say that nothing can ever be changed is, in my opinion, not only an error, but can lead to difficulties in our daily lives.

Let me give you some examples of changes in God's will or plan. God changed the divorce laws (see Mark 10:2–6)—though admittedly this was because of the hardness of God's people's hearts. Sin prevented Moses from entering into the Promised Land and it delayed God's plan for the Jewish nation (see Exodus 3:7–12; Numbers 20:8–25; Deuteronomy 1:37). Man's repentance from sin also may change God's plan. When the people of Nineveh changed, God, out of His love and in response, changed His plan. This resulted in a change of plans and message for a third party—Jonah. Unfortunately, Jonah was unwilling to accept this dynamic change in God's will. Individuals may intervene through prayer and within certain limits affect the mind and will of God. Moses forcefully interceded in prayer for the children of Israel and God's plan was altered (see Psalms 106:23; Exodus 32:7–14). Christ, seeing the need and distress of the disciples in a storm, altered His intended course to respond to them in their distress (see Mark 6:45–52).

The point I am really trying to drive home is not so much that God may change His will or plan—though I believe that may occur—but that *God's will and plan is a dynamic, living, day-by-day, exciting and flexible thing.* If we want His blessing and constant will and plan for our individual or corporate lives, we must be in constant union with Him and listening to Him. We can't smugly rest on yesterday's relationship or direction.

On the other hand, we don't need to become morbidly introspective regarding every activity we are doing for fear we are out of His will or plan. This would be akin to planting a garden and then going out every day and digging it up to see how it is doing. When God directs us to do something we should proceed in that direction. As we are daily waiting on Him and open to His leading, He will direct us if we are listening. If it seems that God is changing His direction for our lives and the reason for the change is readily apparent, fine. We can learn from it; but, on the other hand, if the reason for the change is not readily apparent it is unwise to spend a lot of time in retracing the steps. However, it is imperative that in the final analysis, we know that we are in God's will. Remember, the "man of God" was led by the "prophet of God" to think that God changed His will in 1 Kings 13, when in reality the latter individual lied. The important thing is that in this moment of time we know that we are in His will; and that we continue this attitude during every moment in the future. He most assuredly wants to reveal His will to us if we are but listening.

This is why the attitude of seeking His will is always better than the attitude of having found His will. We must always remember that God and the individual are more important than plans. We must not push people into molds or allow others to push us into molds not ordained of God. We must also be careful that our ego doesn't get attached to a plan, so that if God should seemingly change His plan, it would become difficult for us to change before our fellowman. Remember, the last idol for many is the monument to self which can be closely attached to our plans.

"A man's mind plans his way, but the Lord directs his steps" (Proverbs 16:9).

DISCUSSION QUESTIONS

1) List the things that can go wrong with plans which are discussed in this chapter. Do you agree?
2) Do you agree with the author's "syndrome of the faithful few?" Have you ever been guilty of this?
3) Do results ever vindicate one's life? Explain.
4) Do you really believe God ever changes plans?

5) How can the teaching that God's plan may change be misused? Is possible misuse an adequate basis for denying the correctness of this teaching?

6) Was God justified in making so much over whether Moses struck or spoke to the rock? Why?

7) Can you give a personal example of one or more of the ways described in which God's will either changed or seemed to change from your perspective?

8) Do you think it is very common for well-meaning Christians to hinder our spiritual walk with Christ because of their plans? Give an example.

18

ORGANIZATIONS

"Dr. Carlson, Dr. Carlson, please call the operator! Dr. Carlson, please call the operator!" blared the hospital public-address system as I was making evening rounds to see some very sick patients. As I walked to the nearest phone I wondered who might be calling me now. "I hope it is not an emergency or some other pressure," I thought to myself as I dialed "0." I had started work early that morning; it was now 9 P.M. and I hadn't been home yet.

"Operator, this is Dr. Carlson," I said.

"Dr. Jackson is on the line" the operator responded. Bob Jackson is a friend and highly respected colleague. I wondered what he wanted.

"Dwight?" It was Bob's voice. "The nominations committee for XYZ organization recently met and wondered if you would be willing to serve as secretary." Even as he was asking the question, numerous thoughts flashed through my mind. I had been very active in this organization during the last several years and had anticipated the possibility of being asked to become more deeply involved. In fact, I had concluded that I should decline any office if I were asked because higher priority items were being neglected.

"I . . . I . . . I had already thought about that and had decided to back off this year," I stuttered, as I tried to collect my thoughts and answer in an appropriate way. But before I had even finished my stammering sentence, Bob interrupted.

"Dwight, we want you to know what a fine job you have done the last several years. Your comments at the steering committee meetings are always appropriate and have helped immensely in getting the job done," he continued.

"Thanks," I said, "but I really think I should decline the office this year."

"Dwight, I owe you an apology. We were supposed to get permission from all the candidates nominated but I have been so busy as chairman of the organization and other things that I have failed at this point. Ballots were mailed out this afternoon."

"Oh . . . oh . . . oh!" I again stammered as I tried to collect my thoughts and decide what to say next! And then it dawned on me: maybe I'm running against a strong candidate and will not be elected anyway. That will solve my problem. So I asked, "Who am I running against?"

"You are unopposed" was the reply. I am sure my mouth was hanging open as Dr. Jackson said, "Thanks, Dwight, I know you will do an excellent job. We really need you and it won't take much of your time."

Still stammering I managed to say, "Good-bye, Bob," before I heard the click of the receiver on the other end. I was a little stunned as I slowly put the receiver down and went back to my evening rounds, trying to figure out what had just transpired.

This is only one of at least three illustrations from my personal life during the last year alone, of the pressures that organizations can place on an individual. How many times have you seen a person pressured into a position at a church business meeting or into teaching a Sunday-school class, despite his opposition?

Too much or the wrong kind of organization can be a tremendous problem to our personal lives. Unfortunately, these pressures permeate almost all of our relationships. It is an integral part of the twentieth-century church. Great plans and strategies have been the impetus for tremendous Christian organization as well as the metropolises of secular organizations. Creating desire and need, exerting pressure and extracting a commitment are their common denominators. Christendom has learned and is applying many of the techniques from godless organizations. In fact, often books on salesmanship may be recommended by a Christian leader in order to teach others how to motivate other Christians. Some of these techniques are good (*see* Luke 16:8, 9) and some are definitely bad. Unfortunately, on the surface it is often hard to tell which is which for both the organization and the individual. Only the spiritually mature person understands the far-reaching consequences.

Let me illustrate. Some years ago several zealous Christian leaders were looking for additional personnel to help "win the entire state for Christ." They had a plan, beautiful strategy, and went about looking for the right personnel. They needed a young woman to reach the young women, so called on my wife, then single, to present their plan.

Betty arrived at their office before they did and while waiting for them, she noticed a little clipping strategically placed on the leader's desk. With amazement the caption caught her eye. "How to win men to your way of thinking." As she read the ten points, she somehow felt that for some reason, God had allowed her to read that clipping.

Later as the interview progressed she clearly could see the manipulative techniques these men were using to convince her that she was the one for that spot. Yes, she agreed that not all in the state knew Jesus Christ. "Of course, they should all have the opportunity." Yes, she has a desire to reach out to other women. And, "Certainly, if we all put our efforts together in one concentrated area we could much more effectively get the job done and eventually reach the world, than if we all are doing our own thing in our own little area." However, for some strange reason Betty was hesitant. The personalities and logic were persuasive. Had she not seen the clipping on the desk she might have erroneously thought this was God's will and failed to hear His "still small voice" beckoning her elsewhere.

So here we see that the first and most obvious technique used by organizing individuals is that of judicious pressure and commitment (comparable to closing the sale in selling). All kinds of methods are used consciously and unconsciously in an effort to make it difficult for you to say no. This is complicated by the fact that there are so many great spiritual programs being promoted today, most all of them fully justified and seemingly encouraged from God's Word. It is exceedingly difficult to say no or to voice any negative feelings about the activities of such an organization. To do so makes it seem like we are objecting to the Scriptures or God Himself. Thus the Christian faces a dilemma. Either he supports all of these good programs (which is an impossibility) with frustration and weariness the inevitable result. Or he starts to reject participation in certain programs with possible false guilt resulting. If we aren't careful we may reject the wrong pressures. Not infrequently some people throw up their hands in despair and reject all pressures from organizations— both ones they should and ones they shouldn't. They throw out the baby with the bath water!

It takes a fairly mature person to be able to *properly* handle the pressures of organized Christians and an organized world. At times it will put to the test all the resources of the wise person —whose primary allegiance must always be to Christ. Otherwise, internal conflicts may soon creep in with all their resultant symptoms, including fatigue.

Even conscientious Christian organizations are caught in the squeeze of these pressures. Take the example of finances. If a given Christian organization is competing, in essence, with several other Christian organizations, a local church and several projects, and the total amount available to all of these is limited, what will happen to organization A if it does not resort to the same high pressure techniques used by organization B?

The second technique used by organizations is to meet or create a need. The barrage of advertising beamed our way is aimed at showing us we need a new vacuum cleaner or a new car. If we do not have a vacuum cleaner and are walking instead of driving a car, responding to the pressure may be appropriate. If, however, our vacuum cleaner only lacks the latest gadgets, and our car is last year's model, to yield to the pressures may be very ill-advised. In the Christian's sphere we need certain things that the church and organizations can contribute. Fellowship is certainly needful (*see* Hebrews 10:25). Thus, attending church or a fellowship group may be necessary activity one or two nights a week. But to attend more often than that soon may result in a burden-producing fatigue.

Another way that needs are used to motivate and often manipulate Christians is to emphasize the needs of others. After all, one line of reasoning goes, we are left here on the earth after we accept Christ to help meet the desperate physical and spiritual needs of a sick world. If we are willing to be dedicated Christians we must be willing to give of our time, money—our total selves—till there is nothing left, the line of reasoning might be extended. Christian brothers and leaders may imply that the need necessitates the call to action. This erroneous conclusion leads to a tremendous amount of internal conflict and fatigue, in my opinion. Without a proper understanding of the relationship between the need and the call, many people end up trying to meet every need, running here and there, with fatigue and frustration the result. Contrary to popular opinion, *I do not believe the need constitutes the call.*

For many years I was particularly confused by Romans 13:8 which says: "Owe no man anything, except to love one another." Why should we owe no one anything except love? Then I realized that most of our debts to individuals and society—financial and otherwise—can be met. But the debt of love can never be fully met. The needs and opportunities to show love are innumerable. But this debt will never be satisfied as long as we are on the earth. We, therefore, must learn to live with the needs around us without feeling obligated or guilty if we cannot meet *every* need. At the same time, we must not become indifferent to needs. Satan would like us to follow either extreme.

Christ's concern over the people's needs is a good example. We see Him weeping over Jerusalem as He saw the needs of the people. However, when Mary anointed His feet with expensive oil, His disciples severely criticized Christ for allowing the oil to be wasted, instead of selling it and giving the money to the poor. To this accusation Christ replied, ". . . you always have the poor with you . . ." (Matthew 26:6–12). Luke 5:15, 16 records a time when multitudes gathered to hear Christ and to be healed, but He withdrew to pray. At that particular time prayer was more important than healing needy people. In neither instance did the need dictate the action that Christ or His disciples should follow. Likewise, *the need alone should never dictate our call to action.* The need must be coupled with the fact that *God wants me* to personally meet that need. The person driven by needs alone will be weary, frustrated, tired, and actually insensitive to God.

The third technique, often the actual motivation for organization, is a plan or strategy. I have seen organizations desperately look for a plan or strategy in order to justify their existence. On the other hand, many times an excellent plan or strategy is the germinating seed that develops into a large organization whether within or outside the church. Thus, all that we have said in the previous chapter regarding plans is applicable to organizations.

The fourth technique often resorted to, either consciously or unconsciously, is to think that a particular group or organization has a special inroad or edge on God or His plans. This may be a small group within the church, a church, denomination, mission society, or other Christian organization. This kind of attitude is deadly. A leader may think, "This is the way God reached me. This is the way I started to grow," or, "This is the way it worked yesterday—therefore, this must be God's only effective way for everyone else, too." He may then not only feel that others should get in step with him but may judge those who don't.

The beloved disciple John learned this lesson the hard way when he said to Christ, "Teacher, we saw a man casting out demons in your name, and we forbade him, because he was not following us" (Mark 9:38–42). He was not distressed that a demon possessed a man, nor by the possibility that the man who cast out the demon might not be following Christ. His concern was because the man "was not following us." Christ's reply to John was, "Do not forbid him."

A strong temptation to judge others will come to the person who thinks he has an edge on God and His plans. In all probability he will cause himself and others to sin in the process. Paul reminds us that, ". . . each should learn to see things from other people's point of view" (Philippians 2:4 PHILLIPS).

A fifth technique utilized by organized Christians to promote a plan or strategy is to inappropriately use the Scriptures or spiritual principles. Very often this is unconscious but that does not change the fact that it is a technique that is sometimes heavily relied on. This is especially apt to occur if a person or group starts out with a good plan or strategy and then goes to the Scriptures to support it. Some of our plans are as good intentioned as Peter's (see Matthew 16:21–23)—and as wrong.

Every spiritual truth is not necessarily applicable to every situation. For example, the disciples were told to go into all the world and preach the gospel. Paul rightfully assumed that he should follow this command, so he travelled about preaching and teaching in one city after another—until he came to Asia. To fulfill the command it would seem that he should preach in Asia, also. But the Holy Spirit forbade him (see Acts 16:6). Thus, even the preaching of the life-giving gospel, when not under the direction of the Holy Spirit, can be contrary to God's will. The right plan, however scriptural it may be, is never enough. A passion for souls that is greater than a passion for Christ is really a passion for one's own ego. For those who would indiscriminately paraphrase and use the verse that says, "His word will not return void," let me suggest you study Isaiah 55:11 in its context. There are some definite qualifications that must be met before we can expect God's Word to not return void.

Instead of being a great evangelist, God's message to a particular individual at a particular time may be to ". . . say nothing to anyone . . ." (Matthew 8:4). It may be to go home and live what he believes (see 1 Peter 3:1) instead of talking about it. The point is that even things as close to God's heart as the great commission must be applied in the proper way at the proper time. It is interesting to note that after the command to preach the Word in Acts 1:8, there is essentially no command to the Christians in the churches to evangelize. The emphasis is always on living the life and, of course, in being ready to answer if someone should ask what makes your life different (see 1 Peter 3:15).

Akin to misusing the Scriptures are pat answers and clichés. These seem to have a scriptural ring about them but often are used to manipulate. The question, "Why don't you pray about it?" sounds spiritual but may be manipulative. To implicate our selfishness, if we are unwilling to give, is another manipulative device. The question, "Are you willing to do anything for God?" is a noble question, unless the asker really means, "Are you willing to do anything for me?" To imply that if a person is unwilling to support the work God has given us, he is, therefore, not really willing to follow God, has far-reaching repercussions. Tremendous internal turmoil, confusion, frustration, disillusionment, and fatigue result when manipulation of this type is used within the body of Christ. It may well be a manifestation of wolves disguised in sheep's clothing (see Matthew 7:15; 10:16). After all, if Satan is described as an angel of light and is bold enough to come to the Son of God and misuse the Holy Scriptures, we in Christendom better not think we are immune. Satan will use clichés and misuse Scriptures to try and rob us of energy and soul rest God wants to give us.

The sixth and last technique that Christians organized for action often resort to is "cogging." A cog, according to the dictionary, is a tooth on a rim or wheel. Each tooth must be the same for the machine to run well, so molds are necessary. As a result cogs lose their identity. Webster further says a cog is a "subordinate member of an organization." And a third definition is "to manipulate" or "to cheat."

Like cogs, Christians sometimes get caught up in the machinery of organization, not infrequently losing their own identity and sometimes the reality of Christ in their lives. It is a lot easier to deal with people as identical entities. To treat them as groups having the same needs and responsibilities, results in ignoring their individual characteristics. It is true that Christ spoke to groups of people and often this is God's means of conveying His message to us. However, sometimes a particular message may be the right one for some of the people and the wrong one for others.

For example, all too often a very busy person who gives himself extensively to God's work hears a message on selfishness and the need to give to others. This sensitive person may feel guilty unless he takes on still more activities, thus neglecting some perhaps more important responsibilities that may not have as persuasive a spokesman. This is comparable to my walking into a waiting room full of patients with various illnesses, whose medical history and problems I either know nothing about or ignore, and prescribing the same medicine for all of them. My patients would have good reason to question my advice. Some less mature patients, however, just might take this kind of advice to their own destruction. I could sure handle a lot more patients in my day using this technique and make my life much easier. But what about the patients? You cannot administer healing in that fashion. Just so, the wise leader must avoid excessive generalizing about people's needs and responsibilities. The concerned leader must frequently qualify his statements.

What then are the harmful results of excessive or improper organization? As mentioned above, one's individual identity and close relationship with Christ can easily be lost. The individual's problems and capabilities can by neglect or intent be ignored. Results for a while may mask the deep internal sickness. Often

when things are not going well more organization and committees are promoted. Often there is an inverse relationship between
the sensitivity of an individual or group to the Holy Spirit and
the number of meetings and committees that are necessary to get
the job done. All the internal conflicts described in this and
earlier chapters and the resulting symptoms including fatigue
are the inheritance of smashed cogs.

Why organizations anyway? It is a fact that they are a part
of our modern complex society. The day of the family-run corner
grocery store is past. It can no longer keep up with the imper-
sonal but effective chain of supermarkets.

Likewise, in the spiritual realm, organizations are an integral
part of the Christian's life. An organization, whether it is a home
Bible study, a small group within a church, the local church itself, or a large interdenominational organization, is able to accomplish things the individual Christian cannot. Groups can stimulate and mobilize large numbers of people for commitment to
Christ and service, who otherwise would remain stagnant.

God Himself undoubtedly approves of the right kind and
amount of organization. Moses organized the twelve tribes of
Israel into ruling segments. A certain amount of organization is
found in the early church, as recorded in the Scriptures. Christ
organized His twelve disciples, but even that organization was
minimal. Too often we tend to think that God can only work
through great plans (often our plans) or organizations. This
attitude can lead to serious ego-gratification if we are not careful. Remember what happened to Israel? They rejected God and
demanded a kingdom like other nations around them. So God
gave them a king (see 1 Samuel 8:19, 20). But that king caused
them trouble and weariness.

Organizations can help us get the job done better. They also
can help a person invest his life and talents in work which he
would not have the ability to do alone (see Matthew 25:27).

The crux, however, is knowing how to keep organization
within our own lives, within the church, or throughout Christendom in its proper perspective.

How can the would-be organizer keep organization in its proper perspective? First of all, by realizing that the primary function of the church and our relationships with other Christians is that of fellowship and encouragement and not manipulation, no matter how worthy the final objective might be. High-pressure techniques should never be part of the Christian church. How many times did Jesus use such techniques? Not even once. When James and John (*see* Mark 10:35–45) asked to sit at His right and left hands, Jesus could have told them that if they worked real hard they just might be able to work their way up to those prize spots. Instead, He replied, "You do not know what you are asking."

According to the Scripture, I believe the primary purpose of the church is to provide fellowship, to help the Christian grow and meaningfully cope with life, in a way pleasing to God and to point him to Christ as his source of strength. Reaching out to others should be a natural result of maturing in Christ. Pressuring people into such activities prematurely leads to trouble.

Notice how Christ advised His disciples to recruit laborers for His vast white harvest. He did not tell them to make people feel guilty or selfish if the harvest is not reaped. Nor does He suggest pressuring, using "psychology," or manipulating them in any way. Instead, He said if they were truly concerned about the harvest *to pray to God about it*. He didn't even say to tell people about the need, to drop any hints, to make them feel guilty if they were not concerned about others, but to pray to God about it (*see* Matthew 9:36–38). *Period.*

The organizer who is a Christian leader must also recognize that he wields a tremendous power over other people. The greater the organization the greater the power invested in its leaders. The leader must be careful not to use his power to burden people or extract commitments from them apart from the Holy Spirit's personal leading for that individual's life.

Paul was a great leader and he recognized this problem in the early church. A heated discussion with the apostles resulted.

Finally Paul said, "Therefore my judgment is that we should not trouble those of the Gentiles who turn to God. . . . For it has seemed good to the Holy Spirit and to us to lay upon you no greater burden than these necessary things" (Acts 15:19–28). Burdening others has always been a temptation for religious leaders. It takes thought and effort not to. ". . . nor did we seek glory from men, whether from you or from others," Paul wrote to the Thessalonians. He also said, ". . . though we might have made demands as apostles of Christ . . . we worked night and day, that we might not burden any of you . . ." (1 Thessalonians 2:6–9). At times it may mean more work to the leader in order that the followers not be unnecessarily burdened.

A good criteria for determining whether or not you are burdening others is to ask yourself, "Do I have the best interests of every person at heart, particularly the person I am now contacting?" For example, a leader may have a great concern and plan to reach the physical or spiritual needs of a million people. Then he sees a key individual who can help him meet those needs. To pressure or manipulate the individual into a commitment would indicate that he does not have the person's best interests at heart. He is only interested in fulfilling his own desires.

Everything we ask another person to do must ultimately benefit that person and his relationship before God, as well as the people to whom he will minister. Jonah failed at this point because his ego got in the way. His plan was more important than all the people of Nineveh. To even suggest that another person do a particular thing is to imply that we know God's will for that person. That is an awesome responsibility.

What can the individual do to protect himself from becoming a cog in a machine to his own destruction? First of all he must avoid allowing any person, plan, or organization to become more important to him than God. In 1 Kings 13 the "man of God" was led into error by the "prophet of God" because he listened to a spiritual leader instead of God. Paul tells the Galatians that if he or an angel from heaven came and preached any other gospel, they should not pay any attention to it. No matter how great a leader, church, or organization may be, they are never infallible. The comments made in earlier chapters regarding people-pleasing, the urge to make disciples, and the plan are very applicable here.

Secondly, to avoid problems which can result from pressures or organization, we must be careful about our commitments. This includes not only initial commitments but especially long-term ones, particularly if a person is prone to overload himself with responsibilities. No matter how good the work or commitment might seem, it is usually wise to ask for time to consider and pray about it alone. Too hasty a decision can have far-reaching results. In Judges 11, Jephthah made an impetuous vow which cost him his daughter's life. When a job is being described to you, double the time the person says the job will take. This will probably be a more realistic approximation of the time it will actually take. Ask for God's specific will in the matter, regardless of how attractive the offer may appear or how great the need may be.

Limit your commitment to a specific length of time whenever possible. This prevents you from being locked into a commitment that may turn out to be unwise. Whenever I agree to teach a Bible study or become involved in some other activity, I usually commit myself for a set period of time—say six weeks or six months. This allows other people to evaluate my work and it also allows me to terminate my responsibility if I find it advisable. It is much easier to continue something that is going well than to stop something that is not going so well when people thought it was going to continue (see Ecclesiastes 5:2–6).

If you make a commitment, follow through on it at all costs unless you are convinced God wants you to break it. Occasionally, I have seen an individual who realizes he has unwisely made two conflicting commitments. Perhaps one was made without consulting the Lord. If this occurs, ask God to show you which of the two commitments He wants you to continue. Perhaps He will want you to break the commitment which was not made under His guidance. Perhaps, He will want you to continue. This, however, is not your option, it is God's.

The most vivid example of this I have seen was a man who married outside of God's will. When things got tough he acted as though the decision was totally his as to whether or not to continue the marriage. When you make a commitment outside of God's will, a second move outside of His will never justifies the initial problem. Openly admit to God that you have made a wrong choice, and then ask His direction regarding your future obligation to that commitment.

Despite all I have said, let me remind you that I am not against organization within Christendom. As a matter of fact, I am actively involved in many Christian organizations. In their proper place God definitely can and does use them. The danger is that we may depend too much upon the organized approach, to the detriment of the Kingdom and our own well-being. If we are not careful, we can organize God right out of our lives. I suspect that more would be accomplished for the Kingdom of God if a lot of the energy we pour into organizations were used in direct action under the control of the Holy Spirit. In the final analysis, however, we as individuals are each responsible for seeking and finding God's will for our lives. Only as we are sensitive to Him will we know, day-by-day, exactly what our relationship should be to an organization or its leaders.

Men are constantly looking for better schemes, programs, plans, strategies, and innovations to focus their attention on. This is ego-gratifying. Down through the ages, however, God has been looking for men and women whose greatest goal in life is to be constantly yielded to Him. As E. M. Bounds puts it in *Power Through Prayer,* "Men are looking for better methods, God is looking for better men." The person seeking God's will above all else finds that the Holy Spirit will do most of the directing and administrative work needed. Where there is a Cornelius or an Ethiopian who needs the gospel, the yielded person will be directed accordingly. Such direction by the Holy Spirit can yield a tremendous economy of organization and energy.

OTHER POSSIBLE AREAS OF INTERNAL CONFLICTS

In the preceding chapters I have tried to describe the more common causes of unresolved internal conflicts which produce fatigue. Perhaps only one sentence was directed to your specific problem, but that sentence could be the key to open up a whole new life for you. However, if your problem has not been discussed, face the problem realistically. Use the principles suggested in the chapters which follow to help you resolve it.

DISCUSSION QUESTIONS

1) Why do you think men sometimes overemphasize the role of plans, strategy, and organizations?
2) What was your reaction to the author's criticisms of organizations?
3) Do you think the primary aim of the church is: (a) to help its members grow, fellowship, and experience new life, or (b) to help meet the desperate physical and spiritual needs of the world outside its doors?
4) Do you have an edge on God's plan? Be honest.
5) Do you agree that the need is not the call? How does James 2 relate to this?
6) Do you agree that every scriptural truth is not necessarily applicable or meant for every situation? Give a personal example.
7) Is there ever a time when a mature Christian might know God's will for another Christian? Explain. What are the dangers of this?
8) Is it ever right to pressure someone into something "for his own good"?
9) In what ways have you learned to tactfully avoid being pressured into a job that you did not feel God wanted you

to undertake? What lessons have you learned through these experiences?

10) How and when should a person properly break a commitment?

11) What other areas can you think of that could lead to internal conflict and fatigue, which are not covered in this book?

Part Five

The Solution
(*Energy for the Weary*)

19

CORRECT ANY SHORTS

In previous chapters we have talked about numerous problem areas that can drain a person of a tremendous amount of energy. This energy drain can be as explosive as shorting out one-hundred-and-ten volts and blowing a fuse, or as subtle and inconspicuous as a small short in one's car which becomes apparent only after you have not used the car for several days. However, the dynamics which caused these problems will, in most cases, keep them operative, unless you deal with each problem area in an appropriate manner.

Fundamental to "correcting the shorts" in our lives is *honesty*. Honesty to ourselves and honesty to others. It is fairly easy to deceive yourself if you want to. Jeremiah 17:9 and 10 says, "The heart is deceitful above all things, and desperately corrupt; who can understand it? I the Lord search the mind and try the heart, to give to every man according to his ways, according to the fruit of his doings." To be truly honest about your problems you must have the attitude expressed in Psalms 139:23, "Search me, O God, and know my heart! Try me and know my thoughts! And see if there be any wicked way in me, and lead me in the way everlasting." And then you must look to God to, "Create in me a clean heart, O God, and put a new and right spirit within me" (Psalms 51:10).

The first step toward correcting the shorts is to get the problems out where you can look at them. List each problem (there are usually more than one) on a piece of paper and note what should be done about each. Be careful not to focus on just one problem, especially the easiest one to face. It has been said: "Jumbled thoughts untangle themselves through one's lips or lead in the fingertips."

Four months ago I went through about a six-week period of depression and weariness. This condition had built up slowly, but when I realized what was happening to me I decided to take action. On a piece of paper I listed fifteen different things that were bothering me. Most of them were very minor but each had to be dealt with separately. In the days and weeks that followed I found that some required specific action, others I simply had to commit to God. As I went on to actively pursue activities and goals which I felt were of God, the dreary state lifted as inconspicuously as it had originally settled.

The solution to virtually all unresolved internal conflicts and pressures lies in either *taking action* or *committing* the problem to God. Sometimes a particular problem will require a little of each. Occasionally, the answer will be to wait and take action later. However, often a firm decision must be reached to act or to commit the matter to Him. This does not mean repressing the issue. It involves a matter of the will. Colossians 3:2-5 tells us we must be willing to "put to death" what is earthly in us and actively "set our minds on things above."

Often I hear people say, "But I can't do such and such." Usually what they really mean is, "*I won't!*" God always provides a way out of a difficulty, if we are willing to take it. People who use the word *can't* are often actually rebelling against God and the avenues which He has provided to resolve the internal conflict. (*See* 1 Corinthians 10:13.)

You must also be willing to stop cyclic thinking, which I define as repeated thinking about something, long after it is liable to be beneficial to ourselves or to anyone else. This, too, involves an act of the will—disciplining our minds as well as our actions.

If we apply these principles, we can solve a great many of our problems ourselves with the help of the Great Physician. If, however, we are unwilling to deal with the issues appropriately, if the issues have persisted too long, or if they have become clouded and the turmoil too great, then we must seek outside help. At times God may deliberately choose to help us only through another individual or group. We are our brother's keepers, and sometimes we need one another far more than we realize. The unwilling, proud, arrogant, or self-sufficient individual often refuses help from another person. Thus, he may cut himself off from God's only chosen method of helping him.

Every normal eye has a blind spot. If you cover one eye and look at a blank wall with the opened eye, your mind will deceive you into thinking that you see the entire wall. In reality there is a large spot on that wall that you do not see. Fortunately, God has made us with binocular vision and so our blind spots in both eyes do not coincide. So it is that sometimes we need a second person whose blind spot, hopefully, does not coincide with ours, to help us see ourselves as we really are. This person may not necessarily be any more obedient, intelligent, or trained; it is just that his blind spot does not coincide with ours and, thus, he is able to help us. An unwillingness to obtain this help can prolong, complicate, and compound our problems.

Naaman, a leper and commander of the Syrian army, had to learn to be willing to seek help on the terms available and not on his own terms. He was willing to seek help through the king, but God's plan for him was not to be found through pomp, but through a lowly man of God. Elisha would not even talk to Naaman face-to-face, but sent a messenger. Naaman was told to do something which not only did not make sense to him, but he could think of better ways of meeting the need. His pride almost got in the way, preventing God's deliverance. But a servant persuaded him to obey Elisha and wash himself in the muddy Jordan River (*see* 2 Kings 5). If we really want help we must be willing to seek it any way that God will provide it. Many, unfortunately, don't want help that badly.

If there is any possibility that the problem may be a physical one, by all means see a physician. If, after the physician has completed his evaluation, and you are still not satisfied, request a consultation. However, don't do yourself the injustice of running from one physician to another, accepting only those elements you want to hear.

If your problem is spiritual, ask for the help of a pastor or other Christian leader whose life is yielded to Jesus Christ. If it is a marriage conflict, an appropriate marriage counselor may be God's means of giving insight and direction. If the problem is more of an emotional nature, especially if it is a deep-seated one, the right psychologist or psychiatrist *may* be God's means of deliverance for you.

Often overlooked, but an invaluable source of help to a storm-tossed individual, is a good friend. I do not necessarily mean one who advises or who has had professional training. But it must be a person who basically has his or her own problems resolved, is a good listener able to draw you out, thus helping you clarify tangled thoughts *without condoning or condemning you.* If you seek a friend's help in dealing with small problems before they snowball, you will save yourself untold agony and probably never need more expert help. However, with friends as with physicians, don't run from one to another with your problem, listening only for what you want to hear. If you look long enough you can usually find someone whose blind spot coincides with yours. If you really want to face your problems, find one or two friends whom you can trust and stick with them.

A truly caring church, whether it is two or three gathered together in His name, or a much larger group, can be a tremendous help to the person with problems. Hebrews 10:25 says, ". . . not neglecting to meet together, as is the habit of some, but encouraging one another, and all the more as you see the Day drawing near." And Hebrews 3:13 admonishes us to ". . . exhort one another every day, as long as it is called 'today,' that none of you may be hardened by the deceitfulness of sin." James 5 urges us to confess our faults one to another, and to pray one for another, that we may be healed.

God's purpose is that appropriate Christian fellowship should help us see our blind spots, help us resolve internal conflicts, get us out of a rut (which is nothing more than a grave with both ends knocked out), and stimulate us into further growth in our Christian life. Unfortunately, many of our churches have never experienced this quality of fellowship and stimulation. Instead they have degenerated, through programs and pressures, into an organization that burdens, rather than unburdens, the believer. Not knowing how to really help ourselves, we are unqualified to try and help others.

Remember that the man or woman who walks alone is very lonely, though he may be active in church or other activities and have many superficial friends. In his isolation he does not understand himself and he has no one to turn to when help is needed. He has no one to stimulate him to grow; consequently, he will be of little help to those about him who face deep internal struggles. This man may have all the right answers and still will be of little help to himself or others. (See Ecclesiastes 4:9, 10.) We desperately need to know and be known. We must be willing to accept the slight risk involved in such a depth relationship with at least a few individuals to truly experience meaningful life.

Finally, as we seek to "correct our shorts," remember that morbid introspection can be a damaging and defeating experience. We cannot avoid honestly looking at ourselves as we deal with issues; however, this does not mean God wants us to unduly linger at one point and never move on to greater heights. Correct the shorts, but go on to decide how you will use your energy as you see your potential and draw from God's eternal strength.

In normal health we hardly think about how we feel. The processes of life for the most part operate unconsciously and we are able to devote our attention to other things. Likewise, the energetic person does not devote much thought to how he feels nor is he very conscious of time; he is busy with meaningful endeavors. So we must pause long enough to correct any shorts of unresolved internal conflicts and then rapidly move on toward constructive goals.

DISCUSSION QUESTIONS

1) Have you ever been dishonest with yourself? When?
2) What techniques have you used to clarify and resolve problems in your life?
3) Do you think breaking each problem into either action or committal is an oversimplification? Will it work?
*4) Do you engage in much cyclic thinking? What is it usually about?
5) Do you have any blind spots? What are they? If you don't know how can you find out what they are?
6) If you do not share deeply with others, why will you probably be unable to help anyone else with his deeper needs?

20

VISUALIZE YOUR POTENTIAL WHERE YOU ARE

No matter where you are or what you are doing, your life can have meaning right now. The secret is to visualize your exciting potential and recognize that you can glorify God and beat fatigue in your present setting—no matter what your circumstances may be.

The first step is to see yourself as God sees you. If we all could visualize our true potential as God does, we would probably be astounded by what we see. His love for us would take on a new dimension as we realize that every part of the body of Christ is important—of vital importance—to the Master. Satan often tries to blind us from seeing our potential with thoughts like, "I'm not worth very much to God. I'm not well-educated. I'm not talented. My little bit doesn't count for much." But God, ". . . who hath saved us, and called us with an holy calling, not according to our works, but according to his own purpose and grace, which was given us in Christ Jesus before the world began . . ." (2 Timothy 1:9 kjv), has a different idea. "Therefore do not be foolish, but understand what the will of the Lord is" (Ephesians 5:17).

God has a definite plan and purpose for your life. Ephesians 1:9 NEB reminds us that, "He has made known to us his hidden purpose—such was his will and pleasure determined beforehand in Christ. . . ." This plan includes accepting Christ as your personal Lord and Saviour, growing in Him, learning to love, learning to glorify Him. The details of this plan are individual and personal—details which He will show you step-by-step as you put your faith in Him. In Deuteronomy 30:11–18 we are told, "For this commandment which I command you this day is not too hard for you, neither is it far off." To paraphrase Romans 12:2, you will prove that His will for you is good, meets all His requirements, and He will make you into the kind of person you really want to be.

Frequently I talk with people who feel trapped by circumstances. *They make themselves miserable* by rebelling against their lack of financial resources, education, innate intelligence, their ill health, what others have done or not done to them. All too often the walls which make them feel trapped are self-erected, the result of demands they place on God and those around them. Unwilling to remove these self-erected walls, they become discouraged, rebellious, bitter, and tired. They fail to see that in both the secular and spiritual world people with problems just like theirs have led successful meaningful lives. These people have not succumbed to their circumstances. They may have had failures, but those failures have not stood in the way of their progress.

The Christian need never feel trapped if he will only look up. Joyous Christian prisoners in communistic countries are examples of the peace that can come to the Christian despite his circumstances. Greater responsibility and usefulness come when we faithfully perform the seemingly small task God has given us right where we are.

If you feel trapped by circumstances, take new hope as you read Hebrews 11 and 12. Hebrews 11 depicts the faithful followers of God who, despite gigantic obstacles, were giants of the faith and realized tremendous potential. Hebrews 12 then tells us to lay aside all that hinders, and to look to Jesus, remembering the circumstances through which He went—being misunderstood, mistreated, hurt, and even unjustly killed. We are reminded that our lot is not so bad, since we have not yet shed blood. An indepth evaluation of David and Joseph as well as many others in the Scriptures reveals that they had to live with horrible "circumstances" for a number of years. Despite the problems, they had a tremendous attitude and looked beyond the circumstances to God. Sometimes God disciplines us through circumstances, but this is only for our own good because He loves us.

So often we tend to expect God to change our circumstances. God, however, desperately wants to change *us*. It seems to me many people in essence say to God, "You change my circumstances and then I'll visualize and realize my full potential." All the time God is saying in His quiet way, "You realize your full potential right where you are, and then we will later consider the circumstances." Sometimes when our attitude changes the circumstances seem to change, also. The point is, the only way we can realize our potential is to see ourselves as God sees us and rejoice *in* (not necessarily because of) all circumstances, otherwise we quench the Holy Spirit. (*See* 1 Thessalonians 5:16–19.) "Do all things without grumbling or questioning" (Philippians 2:14).

God's plan is to start where we are as we make ourselves available to Him and turn us into vessels which He can use. When we are yielded to Him, the changes that follow will be natural and easy. If we are unwilling to yield ourselves to Him, we will never realize what we might have been through Him.

Once you have begun to realize your potential as God sees it, the second step is to *eliminate any sin* in your life. The person who harbors sin can never hope to become the kind of person God wants him to be. If your heart is willing, it only takes a few moments to confess your sin to God and ask His forgiveness. If you are involved in a sinful situation from which you must remove yourself, don't think you must wait until every last detail is straightened out before you can start serving God. Ask Him to start using you for His glory right now. However, do not use this as an excuse to linger in a situation not pleasing to God.

This brings us to the third and most important step in visualizing and realizing your potential—*aligning your will* with God's will for your life. Matthew 6 reminds us to seek the Kingdom of God first and He will meet all of our legitimate needs. The more we yield our lives to Christ, the more the Holy Spirit will be at work in us to unify all our desires and activities. Philippians 2:13 promises, "For God is at work in you, both to will and to work for his good pleasure." As we do His will He rewards us with good gifts. The psalmist said, "Take delight in the Lord, and he will give you the desires of your heart" (Psalms 37:4). Remember, however, that you cannot barter with God—"I'll do such-and-such for You, Lord, if You'll give me the things I want." The giving of gifts is entirely up to Him.

As we align our wills with His, receiving or not receiving certain things will become incidental. Often what was once important to us becomes less important. My brother Paul avidly enjoyed living. Yet, while a prisoner of the rebels, he wrote, "Pray not for deliverance but for my testimony." God's work became more important to him than his own life. God may give us the things we originally wanted, or He may change our desires so that those things are no longer important. Not infrequently, what we originally wanted would have proven to be very disappointing.

As we align our wills with His, the work we do will be God's—not ours. This will make doing His will an *exciting adventure*. The gigantic fear of failure will no longer hang like a black cloud over our heads. If at times you seem to fail, remember Samuel who was reminded by God that the people were rejecting God, not Samuel, in wanting a king. The yoke of having to succeed on our own is a heavy one. The Christian committed to Jesus Christ never does anything that eternally fails. Proverbs 16:3 KJV says, "Commit thy works unto the Lord and thy thoughts shall be established."

The fourth step toward realizing your potential is to plan *ex-*

citing activities. Recently I made a list of exciting things I would like to do. I found, somewhat to my surprise, that the list included not only some things that particularly interested me but good constructive activities for God's work, my family, and society at large. One of the items on the list was to learn how to ski. So this winter our entire family took beginning skiing lessons and had a great time in the process. This might seem like a small thing, but out of such small things are the spice of life. Although I will be forty this year, I have decided that no matter how old I get, this is one dog, as the saying goes, who will be endeavoring to learn new tricks the rest of his life—the Lord willing.

I mention this because many Christians labor under the stifling misconception that anything exciting that we really want to do must be sinful. So they trudge along year after year fulfilling obligations with no excitement about anything. It is no wonder non-Christians are repelled by their way of life.

Such an attitude can only stem from one source—Satan himself. The Bible is full of promises that the Christian life as God means it to be lived is full of wonderful, exciting things. Psalms 21:2 says, "Thou hast given him his heart's desire, and hast not withheld the request of his lips." Proverbs 11:23 says that "The desire of the righteous ends only in good. . . ." And Psalms 16:11 promises that ". . . in thy right hand are pleasures for evermore."

The person whose life is full of exciting activities is full of energy. He is never bored. He can run longer without being weary. The tired, weary person has never learned—or has forgotten—how to develop exciting activities in his life. As a result, he is often bored. The most productive individuals are those who have learned to pace themselves with one exciting activity after another. The closer we align our wills to God's will, the more what *we* want will actually be what *He* wants for us.

The fifth step is to set *goals.* It is a fact that he who aims at nothing will hit it every time. Paul says, "I press on toward the goal for the prize of the upward call of God in Christ Jesus" (Philippians 3:14). In 1 Corinthians 9:24–27 he likens a Christian's life to a race which he was striving to win. A worthwhile goal can give direction and energy to your life. "The desire fulfilled," says the writer of Proverbs, "is sweet to the soul" (Proverbs 13:19).

To be effective *goals* must be *realistic*, within your God-given ability, and *interesting* enough to arouse your enthusiasm and motivate you to action. Both *short-range* and *long-range* goals are important. Fatigue develops if goals are too remote. As we accomplish each step towards a goal, we develop a feeling of accomplishment and success which, when kept in the proper perspective, is very healthy. The children of Israel repeatedly got into trouble because they *forgot* the victories won and successes in the past. *Spirit-led success* and a *proper self-image* are very important for a healthy Christian life.

Remember, of course, that like anything else, goals can get out of hand. Goals should guide our lives, not rule them. Each goal must be carefully established under the Holy Spirit's direction with a willingness to change the goal at any time God should so direct.

In 1954 while I was in the navy, a fellow who was helping me tremendously in my Christian life challenged me to think through and write down my goals in life. At first this seemed like an overwhelming assignment. However, I eagerly undertook it. This activity helped me greatly to clarify my course and has saved me many pitfalls.

The basic form it took was:

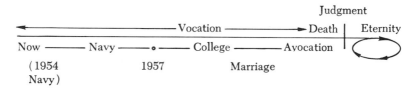

I asked and answered on paper: Where am I heading? Where do I want to head? What is the purpose of my life? How does each phase fit in and further the next phase? What are my short-term, intermediate, and long-range goals? What is my vocation and avocation?

In the ensuing years some of the incidentals have changed—
but fortunately the central elements have remained.

A. W. Tozer says in the *Divine Conquest:*

> To will the will of God is to do more than give unprotesting con-
> sent to it; it is rather to choose God's will with positive deter-
> mination. As the work of God advances the Christian finds himself
> free to choose whatever he will, and he gladly chooses the will
> of God as his highest conceivable good. Such a man has found
> life's highest goal. He has been placed beyond the little dis-
> appointments that plague the rest of men. Whatever happens to
> him is the will of God for him and that is just what he most
> ardently desires. But it is only fair to state that this condition is
> one not reached by many of the busy Christians of our busy
> times. Until it is reached, however, the Christian's peace cannot
> be complete. There must be still a certain inward controversy, a
> sense of spiritual disquiet which poisons our joy and greatly
> reduces our power.

The sixth point in visualizing your potential where you are has
to do with our *attitude* right where we are. "A cheerful heart is
a good medicine," says Proverbs 17:22. Enthusiasm, rejoicing,
joyfulness, and thanksgiving should be a natural result of visualizing God in our lives, knowing all is safe in His hands. More
than that, it is commanded that we have this kind of a positive
attitude. Colossians 3:15–23 tells us to do everything heartily as
unto God with thanksgiving. Ephesians 5:18–20 tells us to be
filled with the Spirit and in everything give thanks. In Nehemiah
8:10, the people were told not to grieve or mourn but that "the
joy of the Lord shall be your strength."

Not only will a joyful, enthusiastic attitude help abolish fatigue
—it will give supernatural energy.

DISCUSSION QUESTIONS

°1) Have you ever realistically visualized your full potential
where you are? If not, why not start now? How can you
get started?

*2) Are you presently rebelling against any circumstance in your life? If so, what?

3) Why should we rejoice in all circumstances?

4) Do you honestly feel that you are as important to God as any of the "great saints"? If not, why not?

*5) Does God have a plan and purpose for your life? Do you know what it is?

*6) Are you really excited about life in general and about some specific things in your life?

7) Give some examples of how a new exciting adventure in your life gave you an added boost of energy.

8) Do you feel that doing pleasurable things is wrong?

*9) Have you ever written down goals and priorities in your life? Recently? Should you?

*10) Do you really believe that God wants the very best for you?

11) Is there anything in life that you wanted and got contrary to God's will that really proved to be best for you? What was it? List the things that you wanted contrary to God's will that have turned out badly.

12) Is there anything God wanted for your life which initially was not what you wanted, but when fully yielded to Him turned out good? Bad?

13) Do you think Satan's biggest lie is that you can't trust God with your life? What arguments does he use?

21

DECIDE HOW YOU WILL USE
YOUR ENERGY

Once you have corrected the shorts in your life and visualized your potential, the next step is to decide how you will use the energy God has given you. Most of us work forty to fifty hours a week, we sleep fifty hours, and we have certain unchangeable responsibilities to family and society. Only a small amount of unallocated time remains. This time is valuable, given to us under careful trust. We often wish there were more of it.

The crux of the matter, however, is not how to get more time and energy but how to use the large amount of energy that has been allotted to you. Fundamental to any decision, as discussed in chapter 2, is acceptance of the amount of energy God has given you, without excuse or apology to yourself or others. Once you have accepted yourself as you are, you must properly channel the energy which is available. If you try to crowd too many things into your schedule, you will dissipate whatever energy you do have. Unfortunately, we sometimes operate under the fallacy that we can squeeze a little extra activity into our schedules without ill effects. In so doing, we ultimately rob time from more important areas, such as time with God or our family, needful hours of sleep, or relaxation, which results in physical and spiritual harm to our minds and bodies.

Several years ago, during an extremely busy time in my life, my wife and I went away for a few days of rest. While we were away I sat down and listed the activities in which I was involved. I was amazed to discover that I was involved in twenty-six specific responsibilities—committees, projects, and other activities. Many were work-related, some in local hospitals. Over half were related to the church and other Christian organizations. Every one was good and worthwhile.

Although I could easily justify each activity, I was forced to admit that my life was suffering from a multiplicity of activities. So I determined that before I said yes to any activity in the future, three criteria would have to be met:

1) It must be worthy of my time on its own merits.
2) It must be worthy, not only in its own right, but more valuable than any other activity to which I would subsequently have to say no. This meant evaluating all my other responsibilities and those I could anticipate for the future.
3) It must be God's will for me.

Then, still using pencil and paper, I grouped each of my twenty-six activities into four categories: PRIME IMPORTANCE, VERY CRUCIAL, IMPORTANT, GOOD.

First were those activities which were of prime importance—those responsibilities which I would have as long as I live—which would not change if I were flat on my back in a hospital bed. In this category I listed my relationship to God and my responsibilities as a husband and father.

Second were the very crucial things. They may not be lifelong commitments, but were high-priority items. This list included my responsibilities as a physician and provider, the importance of Christian fellowship (including the church), continuing medical education, sharing Christ with others, and relaxation. Incidentally, relaxation was virtually nonexistent when I made this chart.

Third were the important activities which included some business and hospital responsibilities, church pulpit committee, board member of a foundation, conference evangelism committee, and our home Bible study.

In the fourth category were all kinds of great things, but considering their relationship to my other responsibilities, I could only give them a "good" rating. (Please note, however—this does not mean that these were not important, nor does it mean that anyone else or for that matter, that I will always place them in that category. My current list looks much different—and much shorter.)

My list looked like this:

PRIME IMPORTANCE	VERY CRUCIAL	IMPORTANT	GOOD
1) Relationship to God	1) Responsibility to patients (and secondarily as a provider)	1) Medical partnership responsibilities	1) Deacon
2) Responsibility as a husband		2) Pulpit committee	2) Sunday-school teacher
3) Responsibility as a father	2) Christian fellowship	3) Required hospital staff meetings	3) Writing personal tract
	3) Continuing medical education	4) Paul Carlson Foundation Board	4) Friday prayer breakfast
	4) Sharing my faith	5) Conference evangelism committee	5) Thursday doctors' fellowship breakfast
	5) Relaxation	6) Home Bible study	6) Office remodeling
			7) Reading hospital EKG's
			8) CCU committee chairman—hospital #1
			9) Executive committee—hospital #1
			10) CCU committee—hospital #2
			11) CCU committee—hospital #3
			12) Bowling league

To my amazement, most of the items landed in category four. Many of these activities were receiving more emphasis than some of the items in the first three categories. After each item I actually graded myself. To some I was giving too much time and emphasis, others not enough, and some needed to be eliminated. Under the Holy Spirit's direction, I gradually weeded out many of the items in category four when the terms of office expired. Since life is dynamic, I am sure group four will fill up again and some will change groups. Therefore, I must continually evaluate my activities to make sure I am investing my energy in the proper areas.

For some people the hardest words in the English language are *I'm sorry*. For me it is the word *no*. I would like to be able to say yes to everyone and everything, but obedience to Christ requires me at times to say no. Like the gardener pruning the vine, I must constantly prune away unnecessary activities if new life is to spring forth. Otherwise, I will droop under heavy vines with little productiveness, frustration, and fatigue the inevitable result. I must be willing to start where I am with my twenty-four hours each day and allow God to direct how every minute is used. Occasionally, an unusual situation will arise which demands our immediate attention, but for such demands God will supply an extra reserve of energy if I have been doing my part to control my schedule.

Some people waste a great deal of energy because of indecisiveness. Perhaps it is because there are several things they would like to do which are mutually exclusive. Or perhaps there is nothing they really want to do. Others just find it hard to come to a conclusion. They remain frozen and indecisive for weeks or months, all the while draining themselves of valuable energy and accomplishing nothing. Perhaps the only decision arrived at is made by default. They do not realize that the risk of making a wrong decision is sometimes less than the risk of making no decision at all, which ultimately is a decision anyway. Not to decide is to decide.

Hard choices are an integral part of a meaningful life. James tells us that a double-minded man is unstable in all his ways. Indecision drains, frustrates and prevents constructive action. It is a form of procrastination. Making Holy-Spirit-directed choices releases us to use our energy to accomplish something constructive.

There are a lot of great things available for you to do in life. If you choose a few and do them well—life will be meaningful. If you try and do them all—none will be truly meaningful. In *Fatigue in Modern Society*, Dr. Paul Tournier refers to all of these great things and pressures in the life as "fragmented toil" and that only a life guided by God will be free from a fragmentation and the fatigue it produces.

In deciding how to use your energy, you will have to limit, not only the number of activities you engage in, but also how much time you give to each activity. Once you accept the fact that you cannot do everything there is to do, you will stop running around in circles acting like you can. Evaluate each of your activities to determine which will be the best investment of your energy. Say no to everything else. Unwillingness to evaluate and choose how you will use your time and energy, under the direction of the Holy Spirit, is sin.

Occasionally you may have several conflicting pressures which demand your immediate attention. Learning to handle such situations properly will help you conserve valuable time and energy. For example, occasionally I may have two or more emergency admissions at the hospital at the same time. Let's say one is a serious heart attack and the other is a bleeding ulcer. Both are my responsibility, both have a life-threatening problem and require a minimum of one to two hours of my immediate attention. Obviously I cannot spend two hours with each patient at the same time. To react with panic will only create a tremendous amount of internal conflict and probably result in poor medical care for the patients. The greater the pressures the greater the need to keep a cool head.

When the phone rings informing me of the emergencies, I first tell the family or hospital staff immediate steps they can take to help the patients. At the same time I can, to some extent, sum up how dire the needs of each patient are and which one I should see first. When I arrive at the hospital I go to the first patient and give him my undivided attention for perhaps just three to five minutes. Then I go to the second patient and give him approximately the same amount of undivided attention. Depending on the situation I may have to see each patient again for say ten minutes before the situation is well enough in hand that I can more leisurely go about my work.

All of us face comparable times of pressure and crisis. We must immediately evaluate relative priorities, then give our undivided attention first to the one which requires the more immediate attention. At the same time we must refuse to feel the pressure of the other situation until we are able to give our attention to it. Pushing the panic button will only result in frustration, anxiety, and fatigue—and perhaps permanent damage to someone or something.

As you decide how you will use your time and energy, be sure to include adequate time to plan, to rest, to reflect, to pray and meditate on God's Word. In Mark 6:31, Jesus told His followers to, " 'Come away by yourselves to a lonely place, and rest a while.' For many were coming and going, and they had no leisure even to eat."

On the seventh day of the Creation God rested from His work. For many of us, Sunday is the busiest day of the week. I do not believe God intends for us to legalistically refrain from all activity on Sunday, but I do believe He is trying to teach us an important spiritual principle which has physical implications. To maintain a healthy body, mind, and soul, one day each week should include a change of pace, a time to reflect, to rest, to worship God, and to reevaluate our work for Him.

The ultimate choice, of course, that will help us make the best use of our energy is to "Choose this day whom you will serve" (Joshua 24:15). Matthew 6:24 makes it clear that you cannot serve God and the world. The goal of each Christian should be the same as Christ's: "I glorified thee on earth, having accomplished the work which thou gavest me to do" (John 17:4); "For the works which the Father has granted me to accomplish, these very works which I am doing, bear me witness that the Father has sent me" (John 5:36); "I always do what is pleasing to Him" (John 8:29).

We can only stand for a very few things in this life, so we must decide *what* we want our lives to stand for and then make the proper choices to achieve that end. When we become confused we need only pause and ask God's direction. He has promised that He will direct us. Usually there is just one thing He wants us to do at any given moment. When Martha was troubled over the preparation of a meal, Jesus said, "Martha, Martha, you are anxious and troubled about many things; one thing is needful" (Luke 10:38–42). God will never fail to direct us in the doing of *that one thing* if we will but quietly pause and ask Him what He wants us to do.

DISCUSSION QUESTIONS

1) List below under the appropriate column all the responsibilities and activities you are involved in. (If this is not large enough use another piece of paper.)

PRIME IMPORTANCE	VERY CRUCIAL	IMPORTANT	GOOD
1)	1)	1)	1)
2)	2)	2)	2)
3)	3)	3)	3)
4)	4)	4)	4)
5)	5)	5)	5)

Now consider each item prayerfully. After each item put a (+) if it is getting too much emphasis, (−) if it is not getting adequate attention, (0) if it should be eliminated, and an *OK* if it is getting the proper attention. Which one or several items should you start working on first?

2) Some people have a difficult time making decisions. Why do you think this is?

3) Do you periodically evaluate your activities? Describe what you do.

4) For you, what words in the English language are the hardest to say?

5) If you have had to say no to someone five times when he or she has asked you to help at church, should this affect your response the next time you are asked?

6) Have you decided what you want your life to stand for? If so, what? What do other people see your life standing for? What characterizes it?

22

DRAW FROM THE ETERNAL SOURCE

I have written this book to Christians who may be perplexed by the problems which they are experiencing within the Christian framework. I have assumed that the reader understands God's personal plan and provision for his life. However, there may be an occasional reader who doesn't clearly understand this fundamental precept and to whom some of the things we have discussed are confusing.

The Bible clearly teaches that God personally loves and cares for each one of us. He is interested in every one of us and wants to make our lives meaningful. The Bible also clearly teaches that our self-centeredness or sin keeps us at odds with God's plan for our lives. The very purpose for which Christ came to the world was to die on a rugged cross and arise again to pay the eternal price for our sin—mine and yours. We can personally appropriate this forgiveness and gift of eternal life through accepting what Christ has done for us and admitting our need for Him. Only then can we know that we are ready to meet God (*see* 1 John 5:13).

This relationship with Christ is fundamental to all that we have discussed in this book. Nothing in the succeeding pages will apply to you unless you first make this initial step to establish your relationship with Jesus Christ. If you have not done this, I would suggest you put the book down, ask God to forgive you for your self-centeredness, and invite Him to take control of your life.

THE WORD AND PRAYER

Whether you have just now accepted Christ as your Saviour or have been a Christian for many years, continual feeding on God's Word is as essential as three meals a day. John 6:35 says, "I am the bread of life; he who comes to me shall not hunger, and he who believes in me shall never thirst." 1 Peter 2:2 says, "Like newborn babes, long for the pure spiritual milk, that by it you may grow up. . . ."

God's Word is our spiritual food. Through it God speaks to us, directs us, and helps clarify the basic principles involved in aligning our will to His. This means we must have consistent meaningful personal intake of God's Word. You can never get it only by osmosis from the minister, other Christians, the radio, or even from Christian books. Without God's Word we will suffer from spiritual malnutrition with spiritual illness the result.

As you spend time in the Word you will naturally respond to God in prayer. Let me quickly add, however, that reading the Bible will profit you little, unless your heart is truly open to God. There is no set requirement for how many minutes you must spend with God each day. You can stop at any point during the day and say, "Lord, forgive me for not touching base with You sooner, but now I am giving this day, my life, and myself to You." However, consistency is important. If you do not set aside some time each day, you may soon forget to touch base at all. Months may pass before you become acutely aware that you are not really in close fellowship with Him. Sometimes it is only the symptoms of unresolved internal conflicts that will bring you back to this place.

No ritual is necessary when you come to God. If you are open, the Bible will bring you to God, but you can come to God even if you have not been reading God's Word. However, when you come to God, He will inevitably direct you to His Word. Even if it has been weeks since you have been in the Word, all you need to do is say, "I am sorry, Lord, forgive me. Here I am right now; I am going to pick up Your step and start walking with You."

One practical aspect I have learned, in terms of starting the day with God, is the realization that *the cement starts to set the night before*. To have a good day, it is important to start it right the night before. I mean by that, having a "clean slate" before God in terms of no unconfessed sin, no unfinished business that I should get done. Before I go to bed, I prayerfully consider the next day, what I will be doing, the commitments, the opportunities, and the possible problems. I then commit them all to God and pray for His divine direction. Sometimes the biggest problem, when viewed with anticipation and the realization that God has directly caused or at least allowed it, can become a spiritual challenge. Though it may take extra time, it need not carry its former dread.

A good friend of mine often has trouble getting to bed, getting up, and not infrequently is tired—especially the first few hours of the day. But occasionally I note a change. He is busy getting everything ready at night, is sure to get to bed at an adequate hour, and has a contagious sense of anticipation of the morrow. He rises at the crack of dawn with a burst of energy that lasts all day—when he goes hunting. From this I have learned a lesson about myself. When I positively anticipate the next day—I have more energy. How we look at tomorrow forms the mold for tomorrow. Therefore, positive anticipation for the day we are living, and for the morrow when we go to bed—in fact, for life itself —will help abolish fatigue and help us tap our vast energy resources. (The anticipation should not interfere with a good night's sleep.)

Another vital aspect is the time I go to bed. I find I must go to bed at a decent hour, preferably having consistent hours. In the

morning, after I arise, I try to spend at least a few minutes reading God's Word and again asking His direction for the day.

MEDITATION AND WAITING ON HIM

The LORD is the everlasting God, the Creator of the ends of
the earth . . . He gives power to the faint and to him who has
no might he increases strength. . . . but they who wait for the
LORD shall renew their strength, they shall mount up with wings
like eagles, they shall *run and not be weary*, they shall walk and
not faint. . . . Listen to me in silence, O coastlands; let the peo-
ples renew their strength; let them approach, then let them speak;
let us together draw near for judgment.

Isaiah 40:28–31 and 41:1

These verses give us many clues as to how to appropriate God's
supernatural strength. First of all, we must worship the Creator.
In *The Practice of the Presence of God*, Brother Lawrence said:

The end we ought to propose to ourselves is to become, in this
life, the most perfect worshipers of God we can possibly be. . . .

It is not our works or achievements, not souls, not gifts. Everything else is secondary. Worshiping God must be our prime aim.

Second, we are exhorted to wait for the Lord. This means not
rushing in to do a job or assuming we know what He wants. We
can easily rush ahead of God if we are not careful.

Third, we must listen to Him in silence—that is meditation.
Paul Tournier makes a major point of this in *Fatigue in Modern
Society*. Meditation necessitates getting away from the busy activities and pace, pressures and problems, needs, noise, phone,
doorbell, and people. These loud voices must be silenced so that
we can hear the still, small voice of our Creator.

Fourth, we are reminded to listen and then later to pray. Often
we rush into God's presence with one-hundred-and-one desires
and even demands; then we wonder why He does not answer.

Fifth, we must be ready to allow His judgment to deal with specific areas in our lives.

Usually it is necessary to set aside a specific time in our busy schedules for meditation or it won't get done. Christ spent forty days with God prior to entering into His earthly ministry (which gives us some idea of the importance of what may seem to some like an unproductive activity). In the story of Mary and Martha, though there were things to be done, Mary chose the one needful thing by meditating at Jesus' feet. This indicates that at times needs may have to be left unmet so that we can draw from the Eternal Source in meditation. (*See* Luke 10:41, 42 and 5:15, 16.)

MOMENT-BY-MOMENT DIRECTION BY
THE HOLY SPIRIT

With our past forgiven, our future sure in Christ, and the awareness that whatever happens to us is exactly what He wants (except our willful sin) or allows to occur, we are free to rest in God day-by-day and moment by moment. This allows us to apply the maximum amount of energy available for the tasks at hand, under the careful and constant direction of the Holy Spirit. We are free from legalism and bondage and can make the very best use of each moment. God has promised us in Exodus 33:14, "My presence will go with you, and I will give you rest."

This constant communion, guidance, or direction by the Holy Spirit is a mystery to some. It does not mean we need to be a monk, or that we are constantly in prayer. It does mean that periodically during the day when I need help or when there is just a moment and my mind is free from the pressing issues at hand, I can pause and with thankfulness to God reaffirm my relationship with Him, my dependence on Him, my desire that He lead me. This brings an awareness (sometimes conscious, sometimes subconscious) that I am His and am being directed by the Holy Spirit in fulfilling His eternal purpose for my life.

Matthew 11:28–30 somewhat summarizes the principles involved in this book:

Come to me, all who labor and are heavy laden, and I will give you rest. Take my yoke upon you, and learn from me; for I am gentle and lowly in heart, and you will find rest for your souls. For my yoke is easy, and my burden is light.

God says that if you are willing to come to Him, He will release you from that heavy burden you once carried and will give you rest. But there is a small price involved. You must learn from Him; you must be willing to be meek and lowly; you must be willing to take the small yoke He has for you. Then God will give your soul rest, peace, and the ability to use your energy more effectively. Then you will *Run and Not Be Weary*.

DISCUSSION QUESTIONS

°1) Are you certain you have eternal life? How do you know?

°2) Do you have a meaningful consistent personal prayer life and intake of God's Word? Describe what you do.

3) Have you ever felt you can't live a spiritual day because you missed time with God? Is that the case?

4) In what ways does "the cement start to set the night before?"

5) How do you meditate? What specifically do you gain from it?

6) What is the moment-by-moment life? How do you start to get it?

7) Explain the meaning of Matthew 11:28–30. How have you experienced it?

Part Six

Evaluation for Action

23

A PERSONAL INVENTORY

Most people who read a book like this only profitably apply a very minute portion of its truths. This can be true even though they may acclaim its contents. The reason for minimal lasting benefit may be caused by reading for head knowledge only, with little intent to actually change. Others want to change but become overwhelmed by their needs and fail to see how and where to get started.

We all need help outside ourselves so that we may decide on a few primary areas of need and then outline a plan of attack. A friend or group is a great asset but if we are honest with ourselves a paper and pencil can do wonders. This personal inventory and solution section can help you get started. If you don't want others to see it—write your answers on another piece of paper. But don't rob yourself of the major benefit from this book by failing to pinpoint your needs and the steps necessary to deal with them. Don't answer on the basis of what the answer "should" be but on the basis of where you are now living and how you feel.

As you begin this inventory pause and ask God to help you be truly honest with yourself, to give you an openness and awareness which you may not have experienced in the past. Ask Him to direct you into the steps of His will for your life.

I GENERAL

1) Is fatigue a personal problem to you?
   (a) Rarely or never _____
   (b) Seldom   _____
   (c) Occasionally   _____
   (d) Often   _____
   (e) Constantly   _____

2) Is the fatigue that you experience usually a:
   (a) Friend   _____
   (b) Trial to endure   _____
   (c) Warning   _____
   (d) Enemy to be dealt with   _____
   (If you answered question one either *often* or *continually* and in question two fatigue is either a *warning* or *enemy*, it is very important that you continue this inventory.)

3) Do you usually know and understand why you are fatigued?
   (a) Yes, usually   _____
   (b) Some of the time   _____
   (c) Often—do not understand why _____
   (If you answered *a* or *b*, list the reasons why you are fatigued.)

   _____

   _____

   _____

4) Are you really willing to change or deal with any area God should direct? yes_____   no_____
   (If your answer is *no*, there is probably little value in proceeding further. Also I would pose the question to you, have you considered how low the Lord may have to bring you before you are willing to see that His way is truly the best way for your life?)

II PERSONAL ANALYSIS

A) Organic causes of fatigue
   (1) Do you eat a reasonably well-balanced diet with fruit, vegetables, meat, fish, poultry, dairy products, and cereals? yes_____   no_____
   (2) Do you have any known illness that is causing fatigue? no_____   yes_____

    (3) Is it possible that you have an undiagnosed illness for which you should seek medical advice?   no_____   yes_____

B) Constitutional causes of fatigue

    (1) After having evaluated all the other causes of fatigue, do you believe your innate energy capacity is:

        (a) Above average   _____

        (b) Average   _____

        (c) Below average   _____

    (2) If you answered *below average,* have you been willing to accept this and adjust your schedule accordingly?   yes_____   no_____

C) Physical causes of fatigue

    (1) Are you trying to cram too much into your schedule?   no_____   yes_____

    (2) Do you have to be busy?   no_____   yes_____

        (If you answered *yes,* do you know why you have to be busy or what you are running from?)   no_____   yes_____

        List:

        _____

        _____

        _____

    (3) Do you often allow yourself to become busy to avoid a truly spiritual life or some other area of prime responsibility?   no_____   yes_____

    (4) Do you often allow urgent tasks to keep you from the truly important ones?   no_____   yes_____

    (5) Do you live or think as if you did not need to abide by God's natural laws?   no_____   yes_____

    (6) Is your activity, Christian service, or the church more important than what Christ thinks of you?   no_____   yes_____

    (7) Are you willing to say *no* (when you should) even if people don't understand?   yes_____   no_____

(8) Is underwork or boredom a problem to you?   no_____ yes_____

(9) If underwork or lack of involvement in meaningful tasks is your problem, is it because:

   (a) You have never seen God's plan for your life?   _____

   (b) You aren't willing to take the initiative and work?   _____

   (c) You belittle your worth and abilities?   _____

   (d) You have some basic problems in your life which must first be dealt with?   _____

   (e) You do not see the dire needs around you?   _____

   (f) Other (list) _____

   _____

(10) Are you convinced that God has a good plan and purpose for your life?   yes_____ no_____

(11) Does your life include a proper variety of activities?   yes_____ no_____

(12) Do you enjoy a proper amount of recreation and fun without feeling guilty?   yes_____ no_____

(13) Do you get sufficient exercise?   yes_____ no_____

(14) Are you overweight?   no_____ yes_____

(15) Are drugs or artificial stimulants a problem to you?   no_____ yes_____

(16) Do you feel trapped in your circumstances?   no_____ yes_____

(17) Does most of your fulfillment and sense of worth come from your work?   no_____ yes_____

(18) Do you maintain a fairly routine schedule (a time to retire, a time to rise, meals, etc.)?   yes_____ no_____

(19) Do you sleep so that you are refreshed the next day?   yes_____ no_____

If *no*, list why: _____

_____

(20) Are you well enough organized to make efficient use of your time?   yes_____   no_____

D) Psychological and spiritual causes of fatigue

(1) Do you have any significant unresolved internal conflicts?   no_____   yes_____
If *yes*, list_____
_____

(2) Are you often anxious?   no_____   yes_____
List causes_____
_____

(3) Are there areas in your life that you know you should work on?   no_____   yes_____
List_____

(4) Do you allow yourself to think about things that you know are not benefiting you or others (cyclic thinking)?   no_____   yes_____

(5) Is there any sin or guilt in your life that you have not adequately dealt with?   no_____   yes_____
List_____

(6) Do you wear a mask?   no_____   yes_____

(7) If you yield your life completely (or if you already have) do you have the feeling that God is a tyrant and will undoubtedly make life difficult for you?   no_____   yes_____

(8) Does any person really know you?   yes_____   no_____

(9) Do you have feelings of inadequacy, inferiority, or worthlessness?   no_____   yes_____
If you answered *yes* put a check mark beside the *areas* involved:

Home _____
Work _____
Social _____
Church _____
School _____
Others (list) _____
_____
_____

Now consider the following reasons that may be the basis for your feelings of insecurity or inadequacy. After each area checked above, list the letter(s) of the reason causing it.

Possible Reasons:
    (a) Not God's will for you
    (b) Lack of preparation on your part
    (c) You are not interested
    (d) You are not suited
    (e) Unjust criticism or evaluation by yourself or others
    (f) You have never experienced God's acceptance of you the way you are
    (g) You have not given it totally to God
    (h) Other (list)_____

(10) Are your feelings of adequacy dependent on your work going well?   no_____ yes_____

(11) Do you consider yourself a successful and capable person?   yes_____ no_____
If you answered *no* make a list of:
    (a) Your God-given abilities
    (b) Past successes
    (c) Areas that you could develop

Now thank God for these gifts. Consider sharing this with someone else and possibly have that person help you with the above lists. Determine that you will start dwelling on these positive characteristics more than your failures and weaknesses (*see* Philippians 3:12–15; 4:8).

(12) Are you bitter or resentful over anything?   no_____ yes_____
If *yes*, list_____.

(13) Do you spend a lot of time thinking about the past or future?   no_____   yes_____

(14) Do you believe that nothing can happen to you outside of God's permissive will (except your own willful sin)?   yes_____   no_____

(15) Do you have a fear or dread regarding your health, the future, or death?   no_____   yes_____

(16) Do you focus a lot of thought and attention on how you feel?   no_____   yes_____

(17) Is there anything in your life you can't (won't) accept?   no_____   yes_____

(18) Do you feel you deserve more in life than you are getting?   no_____   yes_____

(19) Are you living beyond your means?   no_____   yes_____

(20) Are you content with your income and material things? (See 1 Timothy 6:6.)   yes_____   no_____

(21) Do you hold the title to your possessions or have you turned them over to God?   God_____   me_____

(22) Do you use your money wisely?   yes_____   no_____

(23) Is your home a safe place where there is love, acceptance, and sharing one another's deep concerns?   yes_____   no_____

(24) If you are single, have you yielded to God the dating and marriage aspects of your life?   yes_____   no_____

(25) Is sex a problem to you?   no_____   yes_____

(26) Are you compulsive so that it creates problems for you or others? If *yes,* list the underlying reasons to the best of your ability.   no_____   yes_____

_____

(27) Do you have any areas of legalism in your life? If *yes,* list the area(s), the reason(s), and course(s) of action you should take to deal with the problem.   no_____   yes_____

AREA	CAUSE	ACTION

(28) Is your life characterized by liberty and obedience? yes_____ no_____

(29) Do you generally have a critical, negative attitude? no_____ yes_____

(30) Are you often "right" but unloving in your attitude toward others? no_____ yes_____

(31) Are you more concerned about what people think about you or what God thinks? God_____ people_____

(32) Do you see all of your activities as spiritual ones done unto God? yes_____ no_____

(33) Do you find yourself looking to a man, group of men, organization, or a plan more than to Christ? no_____ yes_____

(34) Would you be disappointed if someone you have helped didn't follow in your steps but followed Christ in some other way? no_____ yes_____

(35) Are you bound by plans? no_____ yes_____

(36) Does your ego get hung up on your plans? no_____ yes_____

(37) Of the three phases (adoration, disillusioned, or realistic) which typifies most of your relationships with people and organizations?
    (a) Adoration phase _____
    (b) Disillusioned phase _____
    (c) Realistic phase _____

(38) Are you burdened by organizations, demands, needs? no_____ yes_____

(39) Do you carefully and prayerfully evaluate commitments before obligating yourself? yes_____ no_____

E) The solution to fatigue
    (1) Are you being totally honest with yourself about your problems? yes_____ no_____

(2) Do you need to get some outside
    help?   no_____   yes_____
    If *yes*, list whom_____

_____

(3) Do you have a good friend who
    is willing to be honest with you? yes_____   no_____
    Should you share some things
    with this person that you aren't
    currently sharing?   no_____   yes_____

(4) Are you willing to be helped
    through *any* means God might
    choose for you?   yes_____   no_____

(5) Do you visualize your full poten-
    tial right where you are? (Write
    it out in several paragraphs.)   yes_____   no_____

(6) Have you been looking for God
    to change the circumstances
    around you, when in reality He
    has been trying to change you? no_____   yes

(7) Have you carefully, under God's
    direction, established goals and
    priorities in your life?   yes_____   no_____

(8) Have you aligned your will with
    His for your life?   yes_____   no_____

(9) Are you willing to cut out any
    activity, relationship, possession,
    goal, etc., that God directs?   yes_____   no_____
    List any areas that come to mind
    that should (or possibly should)
    be dealt with_____

_____

(10) Do you ever impetuously squeeze
    in things that take time, money,
    or energy without adequately
    considering the full consequen-
    ces?   no_____   yes_____
    List examples_____

_____

(11) Are you willing to make definite
    choices?   yes_____   no_____

(12) Are your decisions often made
    for you by others, or by default? no_____   yes_____

(13) Do you periodically reevaluate all your activities and prune less productive ones?   yes_____   no_____

(14) Do you need to reevaluate your responsibilities and activities?   no_____   yes_____
If *yes*, fill out the chart below:
Class 1—Prime Importance:

_____
_____
_____

Class 2—Very Important:

_____
_____
_____

Class 3—Important:

_____
_____
_____

Class 4—Other Activities and Responsibilities:

_____
_____
_____

(Use additional paper if necessary.) Now evaluate each of these and put a (−) in the right-hand column for any getting insufficient attention, a (+) for any getting too much attention, and a (0) for any that should be eliminated.

(15) Are there activities in your life that are especially fatiguing (more fatigue results than you would expect by the time or actual work involved)?   no_____   yes_____
If your answer is *yes*, list the activity and why you think it drains you so:

Activity: Why it drains:
_____   _____
_____   _____
_____   _____

(16) Are you sure of your salvation?   yes_____   no_____

(17) Do you have consistent personal
intake of God's Word?   yes_____   no_____

(18) Do you have a consistent mean-
ingful prayer life?   yes_____   no_____

(19) Do you spend adequate time in
meditation regarding:
    a) God's Word   yes_____   no_____
    b) His will for your daily life   yes_____   no_____
    c) Your activities   yes_____   no_____

(20) Do you make it a habit to have
a clean slate before you go to
bed?   yes_____   no_____

(21) When you go to bed, which answer best describes your conscious or subconscious attitude
towards tomorrow?
    a) Dread   _____
    b) Ho hum   _____
    c) Positive anticipation   _____

(22) Do you get to bed at a proper
hour?   yes_____   no_____

(23) Do you live a moment-by-mo-
ment, Spirit-directed life?   yes_____   no_____

Now review all the questions with check marks in the right-hand column. These are the problem areas that need your attention. Prayerfully consider which ones are *most important* and list them below in the order in which you will work on them. Also indicate how you will deal with them. You may want to go back and read the section dealing with the problem areas you have listed. Sharing your areas of need and plan of attack with a friend or group of interested Christians can be of tremendous help. Ask for their prayer, support, and counsel and let them help you check up on progress.

1) _____

2) _____

3) _____

After you have dealt with the above problems (which may take a matter of hours, days, weeks, or months), you are ready for more. Review the column again and list the *next most important* ones for you to deal with.

1) _____
   _____

2) _____
   _____

3) _____
   _____

Repeat this as often as the Holy Spirit directs you to do so. Share what you are doing with at least one other person.

BIBLIOGRAPHY

Bounds, Edward M. *Power Through Prayer*. Chicago: Moody Press.

Butterfield, Oliver M. *Sexual Harmony in Marriage*. New York: Emerson Books.

Carlson, Dwight, M.D. *There's Something I've Wanted to Tell You*. Chicago: Moody Press, 1973.

Cunniff, John T. "Americans Ask Where the Money Goes." *Los Angeles Times*, February 11, 1972.

Dobson, James, PhD. *Dare to Discipline*. Wheaton, Ill.: Tyndale House Publishers, 1970.

Elliot, Elisabeth. *The Liberty of Obedience*. Waco, Tex.: Word Books, 1968.

Evans, Louis H. *Your Marriage—Duel or Duet?* Old Tappan, N.J.: Fleming H. Revell Company, 1962.

Fairchild, Roy W. *Christians in Families*. Richmond, Va.: John Knox Press, 1964.

Herman, Nicholas (Brother Lawrence). *The Practice of the Presence of God*. Old Tappan, N.J.: Fleming H. Revell Company, Spire Books, 1958.

Hession, Roy. *The Calvary Road*. Fort Washington, Pa.: Christian Literature Crusade, 1964.

———. *We Would See Jesus*. Fort Washington, Pa.: Christian Literature Crusade, 1964.

Hummel, Charles E. *Tyranny of the Urgent*. Chicago: Intervarsity Press.

Lindsey, Hal. *Satan Is Alive and Well on Planet Earth*. Grand Rapids: Zondervan Publishing House, 1972.

Miller, Keith. *Habitation of Dragons*. Waco, Tex.: Word Books, 1970.

———. *The Taste of New Wine*. Waco, Tex.: Word Books, 1965.

Morgan, G. Campbell. *Evangelism*. Rev. ed. Old Tappan, N.J.: Fleming H. Revell Company, 1964.

Osborne, Cecil. *The Art of Understanding Your Mate*. Grand Rapids: Zondervan Publishing House, 1968.

Pierson, Arthur T. *George Müller of Bristol*. Old Tappan, N.J.: Fleming H. Revell Company, 1971.

Price, Eugenia. *Woman to Woman*. Grand Rapids: Zondervan Publishing House, 1959.

Sacks, Bernice Cohen, M.D. "Pepping Up the Tired Housewife." *Patient Care*, January 15, 1971.

Tournier, Paul, ed. *Fatigue in Modern Society*. Richmond, Va.: John Knox Press, 1965.

———. *The Meaning of Persons*. New York: Harper & Brothers, 1957.

———. *To Understand Each Other*. Richmond, Va.: John Knox Press, 1967.

Tozer, A. W. *The Divine Conquest*. Old Tappan, N.J.: Fleming H. Revell Company, 1950.

———. *The Pursuit of God*. Harrisburg, Pa.: Christian Publications, Inc., 1948.

Wintrobe, M. M., et al. *Harrison's Principles of Internal Medicine*. 6th ed. 2 vols. New York: McGraw-Hill, 1970.

Wright, H. Norman. *Communication, Key to Your Marriage*. Glendale, Calif.: Regal Books, 1974.